A FAMILY-FOCUSED APPROACH TO SERIOUS MENTAL ILLNESS: EMPIRICALLY SUPPORTED INTERVENTIONS

Diane T. Marsh, PhD

University of Pittsburgh at Greensburg
Greensburg, Pennsylvania

Professional Resource Press
Sarasota, FL

Published by Professional Resource Press
(An imprint of the Professional Resource Exchange, Inc.)
Post Office Box 15560
Sarasota, FL 34277-1560

Printed in the United States of America

The copy editor for this book was Patricia Rockwood, the managing editor was Debbie Fink, and the production coordinator was Laurie Girsch.

Library of Congress Cataloging-in-Publication Data

Marsh, Diane T.
    A family-focused approach to serious mental illness : empirically supported interventions / Diane T. Marsh
        p. cm. -- (Practitioner's resource series)
    Includes bibliographical references.
    ISBN 1-56887-069-8
        1. Mentally ill--Family relationships. 2. Mental illness--Treatment. I. Series

RC455.4.F3 M3646 2001
616.89'1--dc21

                                                    00-047831

Hope is the thing with feathers
That perches in the soul,
And sings the tune without the words,
And never stops at all.

Emily Dickinson

SERIES PREFACE

As a publisher of books, audio- and videotapes, and continuing education programs, the Professional Resource Press and Professional Resource Exchange, Inc. strive to provide mental health professionals with highly applied resources that can be used to enhance clinical skills and expand practical knowledge.

All the titles in the Practitioner's Resource Series are designed to provide important new information on topics of vital concern to psychologists, clinical social workers, marriage and family therapists, psychiatrists, and other mental health professionals.

Although the focus and content of each book in this series will be quite different, there will be notable similarities:

1. Each title in the series will address a timely topic of critical clinical importance.

2. The target audience for each title will be practicing mental health professionals. Our authors were chosen for their ability to provide concrete "how-to-do-it" guidance to colleagues who are trying to increase their competence in dealing with complex clinical problems.

3. The information provided in these books will represent "state-of-the-art" information and techniques derived from both clinical experience and empirical research. Each of these guide books will include references and resources for those who wish to pursue more advanced study of the discussed topics.

4. The authors will provide numerous case studies, specific recommendations for practice, and the types of "nitty-gritty" details that clinicians need before they can incorporate new concepts and procedures into their practices.

We feel that one of the unique assets of the Professional Resource Press is that all of its editorial decisions are made by mental health professionals. The publisher, all editorial consultants, and all reviewers are practicing psychologists, marriage and family therapists, clinical social workers, and psychiatrists.

If there are other topics you would like to see addressed in this series, please let me know.

Lawrence G. Ritt, Publisher

AUTHOR'S PREFACE

A Family-Focused Approach to Serious Mental Illness offers practitioners a concise and useful guide to working with families of patients who have serious mental illness, such as schizophrenia, bipolar disorder, and major depression. Professional practice with these families offers many satisfactions and presents many challenges. Perhaps the greatest challenge is helping such devastated families maintain a sense of hope during the darkest days. As practitioners, echoing Emily Dickinson, we must remember to listen for hope's eternal song, however faint, and to help these families hear hope's song as well.

Because mental illness has a catastrophic impact on families as well as patients, effective practice requires a family-focused approach. In fact, as I will discuss, there is a strong rationale for involving families. Based on robust research findings, for instance, we now know what these families need and how to address their needs. Moreover, there is solid evidence that effective family interventions can also reduce the risk of patient relapse. In *A Family-Focused Approach to Serious Mental Illness*, I will assist practitioners to incorporate these interventions into their practice.

Now, as ever, I am grateful to my three families: to my personal family, my husband, my sons and daughters-in-law, and my siblings and their spouses; to my professional family, the many wonderful colleagues who have enriched my life and my work; and to the caring families who live with mental illness and have generously shared their experiences and wisdom with me.

Diane T. Marsh, PhD

ABSTRACT

A Family-Focused Approach to Serious Mental Illness provides a concise and practical guide for practitioners who work with families that include a member with serious mental illness, such as schizophrenia, bipolar disorder, or major depression. Over 5 million adults have a serious mental illness, which has a devastating impact on families as well as individuals.

Based on robust research findings, a range of empirically supported family interventions are now available that can meet the needs of these highly stressed families. In fact, there is a strong rationale for involving families in the treatment of serious mental illness. First, as is the case for chronic health problems, families often serve in essential roles as primary caregivers, informal case managers, and advocates. Second, families can play a constructive role in their relative's treatment, rehabilitation, and recovery. Third, because family attitudes and behaviors can influence the course of mental illness, an informed and supportive family is a considerable asset to patients and to practitioners. Finally, faced with a catastrophic stressor that can leave them traumatized and exhausted, these families have compelling needs of their own.

Five family interventions are discussed: family consultation, family support and advocacy groups, family education, family psychoeducation, and psychotherapy. All of these interventions have potential benefits for families of patients with serious mental illness. *A Family-Focused Approach to Serious Mental Illness* will assist practitioners in building on their existing competencies, incorporating these family interventions into their repertoire, and designing an individualized service plan for particular families. Clinicians will also gain insight into the experiences of individual family members, including parents, spouses, siblings, and offspring, and become familiar with the specialized services that can address their needs. Relevant professional issues are considered.

TABLE OF CONTENTS

A FAMILY-FOCUSED APPROACH TO SERIOUS MENTAL ILLNESS: EMPIRICALLY SUPPORTED INTERVENTIONS

WORKING WITH FAMILIES

Recently I offered training to staff at a mental health center affiliated with a community hospital. The audience included several medical social workers who provided services to families of patients who have severe and chronic health problems, such as diabetes, heart disease, and cancer. My topic was professional practice with families of patients who have serious mental illness. Serious mental illness has traditionally been defined in terms of diagnosis, duration, and disability.[1] Specifically, the term refers to mental disorders that carry certain diagnoses, such as schizophrenia, bipolar disorder, and major depression; that are relatively persistent (e.g., lasting at least a year); and that result in comparatively severe functional impairment in such major areas as vocational capacity or social relationships.

Following my presentation, one of the social workers commented that my approach was similar to standard practice in the area of health care. A collaborative, psychoeducational, family-focused approach is indeed typical in most hospital-based social service departments. Although such an approach is equally effective in working with families of patients who have serious mental illness, these family-focused interventions are uncommon in mental health settings. In fact, fewer than

1

10% of families that include a member with schizophrenia receive educational and supportive services.[2]

Clearly, many families can benefit from expanded professional services. The Center for Mental Health Services estimates that more than 5 million adults have a serious mental illness. An additional 3 million children and adolescents have a serious emotional disturbance that severely undermines their current functioning and imperils their future.[3] All of these individuals have family members who share in the tremendous losses and challenges that accompany the illness. In the words of one family member, "This terrible illness colors everything — a family cannot escape."[4]

Although mental illness has a catastrophic impact on families as well as individuals, relatively few providers are prepared to offer services to these families. Yet effective interventions *are* available that can address the needs of families themselves and can also assist them as they support their relative's treatment and recovery. My goal in writing *A Family-Focused Approach to Serious Mental Illness* is to assist practitioners who wish to incorporate these interventions into their repertoire.

In this section, I will present the rationale for family-focused services, discuss new directions in professional practice, and suggest strategies for engaging and assessing families, developing a family service plan, and assisting families.

RATIONALE FOR FAMILY-FOCUSED SERVICES

There is a strong rationale for involving families in the treatment of mental illness. First, as is the case for chronic health problems, families often serve in essential roles as primary caregivers, informal case managers, and advocates. Patients with mental illness generally require a wide range of services and encounter a multitude of service providers over the course of their lives. But families are their first and last resort: called upon to fill in the gaps in the service delivery system and to handle crises and emergencies. And it is families who share in the terrible toll when their relatives join the ranks of the homeless or enter the criminal justice system.

Second, families can play a constructive role in their relative's treatment, rehabilitation, and recovery. They can assist their relative to obtain appropriate services and can support the treatment plan. Equally important, during the darkest times, families can offer a life-sustaining message of hope that counteracts the feelings of helplessness and hopelessness so often instilled by encounters with the mental health system. In fact, as I will discuss in more detail later, there is ample reason for hope. Unfortunately, too often new patients are given the impression that they have been diagnosed with an incurable, incapacitating, and progressive disorder.

Third, because family attitudes and behaviors can influence the course of mental illness, an informed and supportive family is a considerable asset to patients and to practitioners. For instance, beginning in the 1970s, researchers found that certain family behaviors are related to increased relapse rates for patients with schizophrenia and other serious disorders. These behaviors — criticism, hostility, and overinvolvement — were termed *expressed emotion*. Additionally, there is now a substantial body of literature documenting that certain family interventions are successful in reducing relapse rates.[5]

Finally, faced with a catastrophic stressor that can leave them traumatized and exhausted, families have needs of their own. At risk for stress-related mental and physical disorders themselves, these families have compelling needs for support, information, and skills.

In summary, then, family interventions have the potential to reduce patient relapse, to improve treatment access and adherence, to decrease family burden, and to enhance social support for both patient and family. Because mental illness is often severe and persistent, providers are likely to have many opportunities to meet the needs of these highly stressed families. Moreover, in an era marked by increasing emphasis on the empirical foundations of clinical practice, there is a solid body of research findings that document the effectiveness of family interventions in serious mental illness.[6]

PROFESSIONAL PRACTICE WITH FAMILIES

Many factors have shaped new models and modes of working with these families. As a result of technological developments, including brain imaging techniques such as positron emission tomography (PET) and nuclear magnetic resonance imaging (MRI), there is now a good deal of evidence that serious mental illnesses are brain disorders marked by alterations in brain activity, chemistry, and structure.[7] In response to this evidence, we have witnessed a historical shift in perspective from the family as a cause of mental illness to the family as a source of support. In short, families have become part of the solution rather than part of the problem.

The system of care that has evolved in the wake of deinstitution-alization and downsizing is as much family based as community based. In light of substantial evidence that mental illness has a devastating effect on families, there has been increasing recognition of their legitimate rights and needs. Likewise, our increased understanding of the course of mental illness has highlighted the contributions of family members to the recovery process. Practitioners now have a range of empirically supported interventions that can meet the needs of these families. These include family consultation, family support and advocacy groups, family education, family psychoeducation, and psycho-therapy. All these interventions will be discussed later in the book. At present, I want to note some of the general parameters of professional practice with families.

A Systemic Perspective. A systemic approach encourages professionals to use a wide-angle lens in working with families, placing the family in its larger sociopolitical context. In fact, the family experience of mental illness cannot be understood apart from the social system, which shapes that experience in important ways. Society defines mental illness and provides diagnostic labels, determines social priorities and policies, establishes the locus and nature of mental health services, and creates the climate in which families adapt to mental illness. Moreover, a multiplicity of forces within society, such as the proliferation of managed care, have a major impact on patients with mental illness and on their families.

A systemic perspective is important in another way as well. As families are nested within the social system, so too are marital, parent-child, and sibling subsystems nested within the family system. As I will discuss later, the experiences and needs of individual family members are colored by their age, gender, and role. In turn, providers need to be sensitive to these differences in working with parents, spouses, siblings, and offspring who have a close relative with mental illness.

New Models and Modes.[8] In the past, many models of help-giving behavior emphasized pathology and dysfunction, fostered learned helplessness, increased dependency, and undermined self-esteem. In contrast, practitioners today are more likely to be guided by a competence paradigm that emphasizes the strengths, resources, and expertise of families; that focuses on coping effectiveness; and that promotes a sense of family mastery.

Reflecting the spirit of the competence paradigm, a collaborative mode of practice assumes a three-way partnership among patients, their families, and professionals. The family-professional portion of this partnership is designed to

- build on the strengths and expertise of both parties;
- respect the needs, desires, concerns, and priorities of families;
- enable families to play an active role in decisions that affect them; and
- establish mutual goals for their relative's treatment and rehabilitation.

As noted, families often serve as a cornerstone of their relative's support system and fulfill valuable roles as primary caregivers and informal case managers. Under these circumstances, a collaborative mode offers obvious advantages. These include engagement in a process of mutual importance, satisfaction with decisions that reflect their perspectives, shared challenges and resources, and enhanced treatment and rehabilitation.

In spite of these advantages, the translation of a collaborative mode into practice faces many barriers. One barrier is the persistence of earlier models of family dysfunction or pathogenesis in spite of the absence of empirical support for their effectiveness. Another barrier is the attitudes, perceptions, and perspectives of families and professionals. These two groups not only differ in training, experience, priorities, responsibilities, and commitments; they may also have had unsatisfactory interactions in the past. Furthermore, their initial encounter frequently occurs in the midst of a crisis, when families may appear confused and distraught, and when overburdened professionals may seem insensitive to family distress.

Important barriers to collaboration occur at the system level as well, including policies that limit professional contact with families to crisis intervention, history taking, and telephone contact. With little opportunity or reinforcement for providing services to families, providers may be further deterred by concerns about confidentiality, which is sometimes viewed as a rigid barrier to collaboration (see the "Professional

Issues" section, pp. 73-84). There are several ways to minimize the barriers that impede family-professional collaboration. At the level of the mental health system, the new models and modes of professional practice should be incorporated. For example, administrators need to involve families in service development, delivery, and evaluation, and to offer relevant continuing education programs for providers.

Individual practitioners can also foster collaboration, which depends on the same qualities essential to a therapeutic alliance. Many professionals think in terms of a working alliance with families designed to complement the therapeutic alliance established with patients. Qualities that foster a constructive alliance with families include mutual tolerance and respect, an absence of labeling and blame, acknowledgment of family strengths and contributions, and attention to basic family needs. Effective communication is also essential to the working alliance, and families should have an avenue to express their concerns and share their observations. Opportunities for questions and feedback should be available so that both parties have the chance for clarification.

ENGAGING AND ASSESSING FAMILIES

Although practitioners may welcome the chance to work collaboratively with families of patients who have mental illness, such opportunities will not materialize unless families can be engaged in the process.

Family Engagement.[9] Initially, professionals need to establish rapport with families. They can enhance rapport by listening to the stories of family members, responding with compassion, and focusing on their expressed needs. For instance, most families can benefit from written materials that provide information about mental illness, the service delivery system, and community resources. In addition, it is important to acknowledge the strengths, resources, and expertise of families. Most families are struggling to do their best under extremely difficult circumstances. Clinicians can emphasize the value of the family's involvement in their relative's treatment plan and encourage their suggestions. They can also assist families to define their level of involvement and to develop the behaviors, skills, and attitudes that can promote their relative's recovery.

Because families of patients with mental illness represent a diverse group, practitioners need to adapt their style to a particular family. Families that appear confused and overwhelmed in the midst of a crisis may respond best to an active and structured approach. Other families may need a forum to express their grief or frustration. Still others may have specific needs or questions that merit immediate attention.

Family Assessment.[10] Family assessment poses special challenges under these circumstances. Especially at the time of their relative's diagnosis, families are likely to be especially vulnerable and to have intense feelings of guilt and responsibility. As a result, they may experience routine requests for information as blaming or chastising their family; even the most neutral questions may seem laden with meaning. For example, describing his experiences at the time of his son's initial hospitalization, one father recalled that the professionals who interviewed him and his wife seemed to be trying to find out how they had caused their son's illness. This retired steelworker told me they cried all the way home, remarking that this was one of the worst days of their lives.

Another family member described similar feelings during her sister's hospitalization at a prestigious university medical center. A teenager at the time, she and her parents arrived for their appointment hoping to learn how they could be helpful. Instead, they found themselves unexpectedly ushered onto a stage, where their grief-stricken family was questioned in front of an audience of professionals and trainees. Tearfully declaring that this experience was the most traumatic of her life, this adult sibling told me she felt like a butterfly under a microscope.

Although both of these encounters occurred several years ago, I regularly hear similar stories from family members. As I was completing this book, I received an e-mail from a father who had just returned from California, where his son had been hospitalized with a diagnosis of schizophrenia. The father told me the staff seemed to view his wife as a "schizophrenogenic mother." When I asked what gave him that impression, he said the psychiatrist told them they should be in family therapy because they were "overinvolved" with their son. This message was directed to parents who had just undergone a desperate search to locate a son who had lived independently for the preceding 3 years but was now missing — and very psychotic — thousands of miles away. The treatment team not only failed to meet the needs of these aggrieved parents, who had difficulty obtaining the most basic information, but also intensified their distress by pathologizing their understandable response to their son's disappearance.

In light of these risks, providers need to take time to engage families before beginning an assessment and to explain the role of the assessment in meeting their needs. An initial family assessment typically includes the following:

- Current issues facing the family, such as the risk of harm to their relative or to others
- Their knowledge of mental illness, including any misconceptions they have
- Their skills for coping with the mental illness and with family stress in general
- Their strengths, resources, and potential contributions to their relative's treatment plan
- The impact of mental illness on their family unit and on individual members
- Other past or present problems that may affect the family's ability to cope with the illness
- The level of support available to the family
- Their immediate and long-term needs and goals

Results of this assessment will enable professionals to respond to any urgent family concerns and to begin formulating a family service plan.

THE FAMILY SERVICE PLAN

Although families may be involved in their relative's treatment plan, a separate service plan is designed to address the needs of families themselves. Few families have an understanding of mental illness or its potential impact. Offering immediate assistance, practitioners can provide information about mental illness and community resources, as well as practical suggestions for coping. They can also encourage families to begin thinking about their current and long-term needs.

Ideally, the initial family session should occur at the time of their relative's diagnosis. In reality, however, as Kayla Bernheim[11] points out, the first session may occur at various points in the family's experience with mental illness. A given family may be seeking information at point A, acquiring specific skills at point B, grieving their loss at point C, and dealing with unrelated family concerns at point D. Thus, there is no single service plan for all families or even for all members within a given family.

Bernheim has described the initial family session, observing that the goals of this session will vary somewhat both with family circumstances, such as the patient's situation, and with professional constraints, such as the time available for consultation with a given family. Nevertheless, there are some general considerations, including the importance of encouraging families to talk about their experiences and feelings. Professionals should also explore the family's previous experiences with mental health providers, because families who have felt neglected, blamed, or pathologized will be understandably wary. In contrast, earlier positive experiences will foster the development of a productive working alliance.

Especially in the initial session, practitioners should focus on areas of strength rather than on limitations or mistakes. Once the working alliance has been established, they can assist the family to make appropriate changes and deal with any shortcomings. Several general subjects are likely to arise during the initial session. Particularly following a crisis or period of hospitalization, pertinent topics may include the following:

- The patient's recent history and current status
- The family's response to these circumstances
- Their concerns and questions
- Their needs for information, skills, and assistance
- Their relative's program and treatment plan
- Realistic expectations for the patient and the family
- The family's wish for involvement in the treatment plan
- Potential conflict with the patient's desire for autonomy and privacy
- Their relationship with the patient's treatment team
- Their concerns about the future

Working with particular families, providers can assess the relative importance of each of theses issues, adapt the content and pacing of the session to their needs, and begin to develop an individualized service plan. The end product should specify the nature of family involvement with the patient and the mental health system, the family services that will be provided, and a schedule for reviewing the plan. For some families, the service plan may consist of nothing more than an occasional telephone call. Other families may benefit from reading material, as-needed consultative sessions, family support groups, educational or psychoeducational programs, or coping skills workshops. Still others may request personal, couple, or family therapy.

ASSISTING FAMILIES

There are many ways practitioners can meet the needs of families that include a member with mental illness. For example, they can assist families to

- help their relative to obtain appropriate services;
- understand and normalize the family experience of mental illness;
- focus on the strengths of the patient and family;
- learn about mental illness, the mental health system, and community resources;
- access resources that can address their family's needs;
- create a supportive family environment;
- enhance their stress-management, problem-solving, and communication skills;
- resolve their feelings of grief and loss;
- cope with the symptoms of mental illness;
- develop a family relapse prevention plan;
- play a meaningful role in their relative's treatment and recovery; and
- maintain a balance that meets the needs of all family members.

As families are empowered to cope effectively with mental illness, substantial benefits will accrue for the patient and family, for professionals and the mental health system, and for society at large.

PROMOTING RECOVERY
AND PREVENTING RELAPSE

The subjects of this section — recovery and relapse — are of central importance to both patients and families. Indeed, having the knowledge and skills that can promote the recovery process and significantly reduce the risk of relapse will transform their lives. I will begin with an examination of the vulnerability-stress model, which offers a useful framework for understanding and integrating current thinking regarding serious mental illness. The model also has important implications for recovery and relapse.

THE VULNERABILITY-STRESS MODEL[1]

The vulnerability-stress model assumes that mental illness involves a vulnerability — or biological predisposition — to develop certain symptoms, and that a range of biological and psychosocial factors can interact with this vulnerability to affect the course of the illness. Some of these are termed *risk factors* because they are associated with symptom exacerbation and increased likelihood of relapse. Others are called *protective factors* because they can reduce — and offer protection from — symptoms of the illness and make relapse less likely. Also important are *symptom triggers*, which are events that tend to evoke or intensify symptoms. Let us take a closer look at each component of the model, with emphasis on the implications for professional practice with families.

Vulnerability. There is now a good deal of evidence that serious mental illnesses are brain disorders marked by alterations in brain activity, chemistry, and structure. As Christopher Amenson[2] points out, much of our current understanding of biological factors in serious mental illness has resulted from major technological developments that have been available only for the past 15 years, including brain imaging techniques such as positron emission tomography (PET) and nuclear magnetic resonance imaging (MRI). Incorporating recent biological knowledge, Amenson has developed an exemplary program of family education that is detailed in *Schizophrenia: A Family Education Curriculum* and a companion manual, *Schizophrenia: Family Education Methods*. When educating families, he often uses slides or photographs to demonstrate brain abnormalities associated with mental illness.

One common finding in schizophrenia research is ventricular enlargement, which may indicate that the brain has atrophied or shrunk due to damage or death of some brain cells. Other brain abnormalities have also been found, including deficits in frontal and temporal lobes, the basal ganglia, and the limbic system. Working with families, Amenson explains the normal functions of these structures, examines the deficits associated with schizophrenia, and ties these deficits to symptoms and functional limitations. For instance, new brain imaging techniques demonstrate lower levels of frontal lobe activity in some patients with schizophrenia, which may have an adverse impact on abstract thinking, problem solving, cognitive flexibility, planning ability, and social awareness.

Genetic factors also appear to play an important role in schizophrenia, based on results of family, twin, adoption, and high-risk studies. In contrast to a prevalence rate of about 1% in the general population, for example, siblings and offspring carry approximately a 10% risk of developing the disorder.[3] As E. Fuller Torrey notes, however, roughly one-third of people with schizophrenia have a family history of the disorder; thus, two-thirds are lacking such a history. Moreover, schizophrenia does not fit existing patterns of genetically transmitted disease and may be most appropriately viewed as involving a genetic predisposition.

In *Bipolar Disorder: A Family-Focused Treatment Approach*, David Miklowitz and Michael Goldstein[4] examine biological factors in mood disorders, including molecular and genetic aspects, the limbic-diencephalic system, neurotransmitters, and hormone secretion. They go on to examine the impact of these factors on circadian rhythms, including the sleep-wake cycle, sleep architecture, pacemakers, and light and time cues. As Miklowitz and Goldstein discuss, the vulnerability-stress model works equally well in providing patient and family education in mood disorders.

Symptoms and Limitations. Although there is significant individual variability, these neurobiological deficits are associated with certain symptoms and limitations. Depending on diagnosis, the symptoms of mental illness may include the following:

- Positive (psychotic) symptoms, such as hallucinations, delusions, disorganized thought and speech, and bizarre behavior
- Negative symptoms, which are characterized by a decline in normal thoughts, experiences, and feelings (e.g., lack of motivation or of pleasure)
- Disturbances of mood, including severely depressed mood, unusually elevated mood, or extreme mood swings
- Potentially harmful or self-destructive behavior

- Socially inappropriate or disruptive behavior
- Poor daily living habits

As patients assume responsibility for managing their illness, it is essential for them to identify their symptoms, develop effective symptom management strategies, and monitor their symptoms for signs of impending relapse.

In addition to symptoms, certain limitations are associated with serious mental illness, including unusual vulnerability to environmental and interpersonal stress, as well as deficiencies in cognitive and social functioning.

Risk and Protective Factors. As noted, a range of biological and psychosocial factors can interact with biologically based vulnerability to affect the course of serious mental illness. Risk factors increase the likelihood that symptoms will worsen or that a relapse will occur. Examples of risk factors include increased stress, substance use, and an unhealthy lifestyle. Patients can reduce their risk factors and enhance their prospects for recovery by developing good stress-management skills, avoiding alcohol and street drugs, and maintaining regular eating and sleeping patterns. When increased exposure to a risk factor is unavoidable, such as the stress associated with a new job, patients can at least anticipate and prepare for possible problems.

Protective factors can reduce symptoms of the illness and make relapse less likely. Examples of such factors include medication, coping skills, and family and social support. For instance, based on his meta-analysis of research findings, Ian Falloon and his colleagues[5] concluded that appropriate medication can decrease symptoms in 75% of patients with schizophrenia, reducing their risk of relapse from 70% to 30%-40%. Medication can also increase their response to other interventions. Patients can strengthen their protective factors and improve their prospects for recovery by following their medication regime, developing effective coping skills, and expanding their support network, perhaps by participating in a consumer support group or drop-in center.

Symptom Triggers. As mentioned earlier, certain events seem to trigger symptoms, almost as if a button is pushed and the symptoms get turned on. These events — the buttons that are pushed — are sometimes called symptom triggers. Symptom triggers may be related to medication (e.g., skipping doses, stopping medication, changing medication, or taking other medication); to use of alcohol and street drugs; and to excessive stress (e.g., overstimulation or excessive change). Other triggers may involve medical problems, the illness cycle itself, interpersonal conflict, or lifestyle issues. As with risk factors, once patients have identified their personal symptom triggers, they can avoid them or at least reduce their exposure.

Implications for Families. The preceding discussion has important implications for professional practice with families. As families become familiar with current biological research findings, their debilitating feelings of guilt and responsibility are likely to diminish. Families can also benefit from education about the symptoms and functional limitations associated with the illness; about risk and protective factors that can affect the course of the illness; and about helpful skills and adaptations. Implementing their knowledge of the vulnerability-stress model, families can assist their relative to minimize risk factors, strengthen protective factors, and avoid symptom triggers. They are also likely to gain insight into the role of medication, which can control the symptoms of mental illness, and of psychosocial interventions designed to improve stress-management skills, cognitive functioning, and social competence.

As Harriet Lefley[6] has discussed, families should be educated about the limitations associated with mental illness, including their relative's potential cognitive and social deficiencies as well as his or her unusual vulnerability to stress. Falloon and his colleagues[7] estimate that interpersonal environments characterized by hostility, overinvolvement, and criticism (the "expressed emotion" mentioned earlier) increase the risk of future relapses three to four times. As families become better informed about these issues, they will understand the need to enhance their communication and problem-solving skills, maintain a low-stress environment, and develop appropriate expectations for their relative. More positively, families also want to learn how they can facilitate their relative's recovery process.

PROMOTING RECOVERY

Recovery is the hallmark of effective treatment and rehabilitation. Yet our understanding of the recovery process in serious mental illness comes primarily from the personal accounts of people with mental illness themselves,[8] who variously refer to themselves as *consumers, survivors,* or *ex-patients* (or as *consumer/survivors*). As important as recovery is to patients and their families, the concept remains an elusive one. Patricia Deegan[9] has described her recovery as a "journey of the heart," remarking that recovery does not mean cure; rather, it is an attitude, a stance, and a way of approaching the day's challenges. Another consumer/survivor has defined recovery as developing new meaning and purpose in one's life: "Recovery is a deeply personal and unique process of changing one's attitudes, values, self-concept, and goals. It is finding ways to live a hopeful, satisfying, active, and contributing life."[10]

Perspectives on Recovery. Based on the literature of personal accounts and the relatively few empirical studies available, it is clear that recovery is a process, not an outcome. Nor, as Deegan asserts, does recovery require a cure or an absence of symptoms. Rather, recovery involves a way of living that allows individuals to move beyond the illness in creating a meaningful and satisfying life. Placed in perspective, mental illness becomes simply one life experience that neither defines individuals nor places artificial limits on their lives.

Recovery is often associated with the idea of empowerment, a transformational experience that involves reclaiming, redefining, and rebuilding one's life in the wake of mental illness. The emphasis is on thriving as opposed to merely surviving, and on quality of life as opposed to symptom control. The literature of personal accounts underscores the importance of regaining hope, taking charge, and making choices. Clearly, it is consumer/survivors themselves who are the architects of their own recovery.

In connection with Boston University's Recovery Research Project, Cheryl Gagne[11] conducted extensive interviews with people who had been diagnosed with mental illness. Asked what they were recovering from, these consumer/survivors provided the following answers: loss of self and hope; loss of connection; loss of roles and opportunities; multiple and recurring traumas; devaluing and disempowering programs, practices, and environments; and stigma and discrimination in society.

Gagne identified four phases of recovery: (a) overwhelmed by the disability, (b) struggling with the disability, (c) living with the disability, and (d) living beyond the disability. She also discussed the barriers and facilitators of recovery at each stage. Barriers to recovery include persistence of symptoms, lack of access to helpful treatment, devaluing experiences, recurring trauma, feelings of hopelessness and powerlessness, low expectations of others, lack of opportunity for valued roles, lack of connection to others, stigma and shame, and financial insecurity. Facilitators of recovery include hope, good treatment, social support, coping/relapse management/self-care skills, therapy, satisfying and meaningful work, connections with others, and spiritual connections.

Hope is arguably the most vital factor in recovery, yet the initial encounter with the mental health system frequently instills feelings of helplessness and hopelessness instead. In fact, recovery from serious mental illness, once thought impossible, has been repeatedly documented in long-term studies that suggest a life process open to multiple influences and characterized by many outcomes, a majority of them positive.[12] Lifetime recovery can be anticipated for at least two-thirds of those who are diagnosed with serious mental illness.[13] Recovery is also manifested in the productive lives of an increasing number of recovered and recovering people who are open about their experience.[14] Two eloquent examples of such personal accounts are *An Unquiet Mind: A Memoir of Moods and Madness* by Kay Redfield Jamison and *Darkness Visible: A Memoir of Madness* by William Styron.

Consumer/survivors offer many suggestions for promoting recovery, repeatedly affirming the importance of other people — professionals, family, and friends — who can offer love, comfort, validation, communion, and hope. Similarly, as a "culture of healing,"[15] self-help groups can provide practical information, insight, and support; a comfortable means of coming to accept and deal with mental illness; and life-enhancing hope. In Deegan's[16] words, "During the dark night of anguish and despair when individuals live without hope, the presence of other persons in recovery can challenge that despair through example."

The Role of Treatment. Certainly, the recovery process depends on the personal qualities of consumers: on their courage, persistence, and resilience. Equally true, advances in mental health treatment have played an important role, including new pharmacological and psychosocial interventions, either singly or in combination. In the case of schizophrenia, in addition to the benefits obtained by optimal pharmacotherapy, family intervention further reduces the risk of relapse two to threefold.[17] Effective interventions, including family interventions, are also available for bipolar disorder and major depression.[18]

As reported in a government document,[19] treatment outcomes for serious mental illness compare favorably with those of general medical problems. Following short-term treatment, the percentage of patients improved (reduction of symptoms) was 60% for schizophrenia, 80% for bipolar disorder, and 65% for major depression. Similarly, 1-year relapse rates differed significantly between active treatment and placebo groups for schizophrenia (25% vs. 80%), bipolar disorder (34% vs. 81%), and major depression (18% vs. 65%).

In spite of the availability of effective treatment, in a government survey,[20] only 29% of patients with serious mental illness reported that they were seen by a mental health specialist during the previous year. Likewise, the Schizophrenia Patient Outcomes Research Team (PORT)[21] reported that the following recommended treatments are being received by only a minority of patients: an appropriate dose of ongoing medication (29.1% of patients); medication for side effects (46.1%); antidepressant medication (45.7%); psychotherapy (45.0%); family education and support (9.6%); vocational rehabilitation (22.5%); and Assertive Community Treatment (10.1%). This lack of satisfactory — or indeed, any — treatment has devastating consequences for these patients, for their families, and for society.

PREVENTING RELAPSE

If recovery is envisioned as the process of constructing a meaningful and satisfying life in which symptoms, if present, are in the background, then relapse is its opposite. Serious mental illness is typically marked by periods of remission, when there are few symptoms, and of exacerbation, when symptoms become much worse. Relapse is usually defined as an exacerbation or intensification of symptoms severe enough to interfere with daily living activities.[22] Relapses are often associated with an increased risk of hospitalization, loss of energy and pleasure in life, and the return of feelings of hopelessness. In short, the illness takes over. Clearly, relapses are significant barriers to recovery.

In the past, professionals, patients, and families alike often thought of relapses like lightning. Like lightning, relapses seemed to strike suddenly, without warning, often causing a good deal of damage. Each exacerbation intensified the feelings of helplessness experienced by patients, who were given little reason to believe that relapses could be predicted or prevented. But as any meteorologist can attest, based on information about the weather, we can now do a reasonably good job of predicting lightning. And we now know that relapses often *can* be predicted — and that most of them *can* be prevented.

In fact, in *Family Skills in Relapse Prevention*, Amenson[23] estimates that as many as 80% of relapses may be preventable. Unquestionably, then, it makes sense for practitioners to focus on preventing relapse. Such an approach is likely to reduce the risk of costly hospitalizations as well as the traumatic disruption of individual and family lives. Although assisting patients and families to develop relapse prevention skills requires more professional time than pharmacotherapy alone, researchers have shown that over the course of a year, substantial professional time is saved through reductions in crisis management and hospital care.[24]

As Amenson[25] observes, many variables can affect relapse, including illness variables (e.g., history, symptoms, treatment responsiveness); patient variables (e.g., prior level of functioning, personality style, acceptance of the illness, treatment adherence, coping strategies, substance use); system variables (e.g., service availability and adequacy); and family variables (e.g., level of support, quality of family environment). A majority of these variables can be modified by an effective relapse prevention plan. Furthermore, as Amenson discusses, it has become clear that relapse occurs in stages, each of which has important implications for patient and family education.

STAGES OF RELAPSE

Adapted from Amenson's[26] stages-of-relapse model, the table on page 19 presents five stages, each with its characteristics and strategies. The stages include Stability, Early Warning Signs, Relapse, Symptom Remission, and Recovery. Significantly, most relapses can be avoided if patients learn to maintain stability (in Stage 1) and to respond to early warning signs (in Stage 2).

The stages-of-relapse model has important implications for families. As already noted, families can reduce the risk of patient relapse by providing a supportive and low-stress environment. In addition, they can play an important role during each stage of relapse and recovery. During Stage 1, families can assist their relative to maintain a healthy lifestyle; to manage symptoms and side effects of medication; to develop good coping and interpersonal skills; and to monitor symptom

TABLE 1: STAGES OF RELAPSE

Stages	Characteristics	Strategies
Stage 1: Stability	• Symptoms controlled • Mental illness in background • Satisfactory quality of life	• Maintain healthy lifestyle • Manage symptoms and side effects of medication • Use good coping and interpersonal skills • Chart triggers/symptoms/warning signs
Stage 2: Early Warning Signs	• Return or increase of symptoms • Anxious and overwhelmed • Changes in behavior • Changes in biological rhythms • Concern of others	• Recognize warning signs (93% relatives; 70% consumers) • Chart symptoms • Respond quickly (most relapses take 2 or more weeks) • Contact case manager, therapist, and so on • Modify treatment plan as needed
Stage 3: Relapse	• Runs its course • Severe symptoms • Loss of control	• Obtain relief, protection, and treatment • Maintain hope and heart (usually 1-2 weeks)
Stage 4: Symptom Remission	• Quiet, passive, and dazed • Aftermath of trauma	• Follow treatment regime • Be patient (approximately 2-6 weeks)
Stage 5: Recovery	• Skill recovery (often 6-9 months) • Healing and reintegration • High risk for relapse	• Be patient • Manage symptoms and symptom triggers • Monitor risk factors • Enhance protective factors

triggers, symptoms, and warning signs. During Stage 2, they can encourage the patient to chart symptoms, to respond to warning signs, and to contact the case manager or therapist as appropriate. These strategies can significantly reduce the risk of relapse.

Once relapse has occurred, during Stages 3 and 4, families can assist the patient to obtain appropriate treatment and to follow the treatment regime. Families also need to maintain a sense of hope and to communicate their hopefulness to the patient. During Stages 4 and 5, the patient remains at high risk for another relapse, so families should remain supportive and encourage their relative to develop realistic plans for the present and the future. More formally, practitioners can work with patients and their families to develop a relapse prevention plan.

A RELAPSE PREVENTION PLAN

An effective relapse prevention plan includes several elements already discussed. These include identifying, managing, and monitoring symptoms; minimizing personal risk factors; strengthening personal protective factors; and avoiding personal symptom triggers. Patients and families also need to identify warning signs that can signal an impending relapse. In fact, Amenson reports that 93% of family members and 70% of patients are able to identify warning signs. All of these strategies are contained in the following relapse prevention plan (Table 2), which is designed for patients. The nature of family involvement will vary with their role in the patient's life. Parents who are serving as primary caregivers for an adult child who is residing at home should be

---

TABLE 2: RELAPSE PREVENTION PLAN

---

1. *Maintain Wellness:*
   - Get sufficient sleep
   - Develop good eating habits
   - Find time for exercise and relaxation
   - Build satisfying relationships
   - Participate in meaningful activities

2. *Take Charge:*
   - Learn about mental illness
   - Become involved in your treatment
   - Join a consumer-run program
   - Become active in advocacy
   - Make responsible choices

3. *Apply the Vulnerability-Stress Model:*
   - Understand vulnerability
   - Learn symptom management
   - Identify and minimize risk factors
   - Strengthen protective factors
   - Avoid symptom triggers

4. *Manage Your Medication:*
   - Be familiar with your medication
   - Take as prescribed
   - Understand its role in treatment
   - Cope with side effects
   - Communicate with your physician

5. *Develop Your Coping Skills:*
   - Avoid stressful people and situations
   - Improve stress-management skills
   - Develop problem-solving skills
   - Use good communication skills
   - Express needs assertively

6. *Expand Your Support Network:*
   - Family
   - Friends
   - Consumers
   - Companion
   - Providers

7. *Recognize Your Warning Signs:*
   - Increase in daily symptoms
   - Return of former symptoms
   - Changes in feelings or behavior
   - Changes in biological rhythms
   - Concern of others

8. *Keep a Daily Record:*
   - Chart symptoms and warning signs
   - Rating scale: 1 = absent, 2 = slight, 3 = moderate, 4 = severe
   - Note worsening and returning symptoms
   - Note changes in warning signs

9. *Develop a Personal Action Plan:*
   - Make a list of names and phone numbers
   - Write directions to the clinic
   - Decide who and when to contact
   - Identify a support person
   - Give copies of plan to all parties

10. *Conduct a Relapse Drill:*
    - Review Steps 1 through 9
    - Discuss possible responses
    - Evaluate and select strategies
    - Assign roles and responsibilities
    - Plan for future implementation

11. *Respond to Warning Signs:*
    - Pull back for a while
    - Participate in calming activities
    - Reach out to others
    - Temporarily adjust expectations
    - Maintain daily routine and structure

12. *Cultivate a Personal Garden:*
    - Nourish your talents
    - Explore your interests
    - Seek out new people and opportunities
    - Make lifestyle changes
    - Contribute your gifts

involved in developing and implementing the plan. Other family members may play less active but still supportive roles.

In addition to Amenson's publications, the relapse prevention plan draws from several other resources.[27] These include *Living Without Depression and Manic Depression: A Workbook for Maintaining Mood Stability* by Mary Ellen Copeland; *Bipolar Disorder: A Family-Focused Treatment Approach* by David Miklowitz and Michael Goldstein; "The Three R's Rehabilitation Program" developed by Mary Moller and Milene Murphy; *Behavioral Family Therapy for Psychiatric Disorders* by Kim Mueser and Shirley Glynn; and *Team Care Solutions*, edited by Peter Weiden.

THE FAMILY EXPERIENCE OF MENTAL ILLNESS

To work effectively with families, practitioners need to understand their experience of mental illness. Families are much like mobiles, those unique works of sculpture that consist of wire and colored shapes. When one person develops mental illness, it sets the whole family mobile in motion and affects each of its members. For patients and families alike, mental illness is truly a transformational event — one of those rare pivotal experiences that seem to demarcate life into "before" and "after." Now well charted by researchers, the family experience of mental illness is often described in terms of family burden, family resilience, family diversity, and family adaptation. I will discuss each of these topics, as well as mediating variables and family risks.

FAMILY BURDEN

Professionals often refer to the impact of mental illness on families in terms of family or caregiver burden, which is the overall level of distress resulting from the illness.[1] Sometimes the burden is separated into subjective burden, which is the personal suffering experienced by family members, and objective burden, which is the practical problems and hardships associated with the illness. Whatever the label, however, these shared family experiences are imbued with a sense of torment and despair. Speaking for legions of family members, one mother wrote, "In the dark soul of the night, I grieve for all of us: for the anguish of the past and the present, and for the uncertainty of the future."

Subjective Burden. In telling their stories, family members often speak of their feelings of grief and loss. Indeed, at the nucleus of the family experience is a powerful grieving process that may include their most cherished hopes and dreams. Family members may mourn for the person they knew before the onset of the illness, for the anguish of their family, and for their personal losses. One adult offspring lamented her "loss of a healthy mother, a normal childhood, and a stable home."

As families come to terms with the mental illness, they rarely move smoothly through a series of stages that culminate in a state of serene acceptance. In reality, families are likely to experience continuing feelings of grief that wax and wane over a lifetime — what has been called *chronic sorrow.*[2] Often, this anguish is woven into the familial fabric on a continuing basis, with the potential for periodic emotional firestorms. In the words of one family member, "It's like someone close died, but there's no closure. It's never over."

As their stories attest, families sometimes feel they are riding an emotional roller coaster in response to the periods of relapse and remission that typically mark the course of mental illness. These cycles create considerable turmoil for family members, who often experience intense distress when renewed hope is shattered by another crisis or hospitalization. A mother said her daughter's relapse felt "like a small death," as if she herself were more vulnerable for having dared to hope again.

Over time — and usually with considerable difficulty — most family members do come to terms with the mental illness and move on with their lives. Yet many continue to experience empathic pain for the continuing losses of their beloved relative and their beleaguered family. One mother spoke of her devastation at seeing her daughter "so crushed and destroyed and broken"; another remarked that her family had "lost its *joie de vivre* someplace along the way."

Objective Burden. This subjective burden is accompanied by an equally weighty objective burden: the family's daily hassles and periodic crises. Along with the symptoms of the illness, families must cope with their caregiving responsibilities, family disruption and stress, the limitations of the service delivery system, and social stigma. Depending on their relative's diagnosis, family members may have to cope with positive and negative symptoms, disturbances of mood, potentially harmful or self-destructive behavior, socially inappropriate or disruptive behavior, and poor daily living habits. Unquestionably, these symptoms have the greatest impact on people with mental illness themselves, but families also share the onus.

As Lefley[3] has discussed, family members, assuming roles for which they are unprepared and untrained, gradually learn to cope with the requirements of daily life with someone who has mental illness; to obtain services from the mental health, welfare, and medical systems; and perhaps to negotiate with the legal and criminal justice systems. A substantial price is paid for caregiving by family members, especially mothers, who may sacrifice their own life plans. As one mother related, "My daughter's mental illness pushed us back into parenting of the most demanding kind, probably for the rest of our lives."

Disruption and stress are an intrinsic part of the family experience of mental illness. At least periodically, families are likely to be faced with household disarray, financial difficulties, employment problems, strained marital and family relationships, challenges to their own physical and mental health, and diminished social life. When they experience these problems on a continuing basis, with little opportunity for respite — as many families do — exhaustion and burnout are virtually inevitable.

With ample reason, families worry that their relative will experience homelessness, incarceration, isolation and abuse, life-threatening accidents and injuries, and untreated medical problems. In fact, the specter of harm is a reality for families whose relatives confront a death rate from suicide and other causes of death that is significantly higher than the rate of the general population.[4] Moreover, there are as many people with mental illness residing in our jails and prisons as in all of our hospitals, and at least one-third of the homeless are estimated to have a mental illness.[5] As one sibling remarked, "I see my brother in every disheveled and disoriented homeless person."

Although the great majority of people with mental illness are no more dangerous than the general population, a substantial minority may indeed be more violent, including those who fail to receive treatment or have a concurrent substance abuse problem.[6] When it does occur, violence is often directed at family members, particularly mothers who reside with the patient.[7] The challenge is to acknowledge the real risks for these family members while countering the stereotypical exaggeration of violence in the media.

Patients with mental illness often require a wide range of mental health, physical health, social, rehabilitative, vocational, and residential services. Unfortunately, these services are not always available; nor are they always satisfactory when they *are* available. Families complain about the absence of treatment for large numbers of people with serious mental illness, the relative neglect of patients with the most severe and persistent problems, inadequate funding for the full range of community-based services, and fragmentation of existing services.[8]

Additionally, professional services are often lacking for families themselves, who often report unsatisfactory handling of crises and emergencies, insufficient communication and availability on the part of professionals, an absence of programs and services for families, and limited involvement of families in treatment planning.[9] As noted earlier, the Schizophrenia Patient Outcomes Research Team (PORT)[10] found that fewer than 10% of families receive even minimal educational and supportive services. As a family member declared, "Caring families get socked with most of the responsibility and blame but little legal or therapeutic support."

For many families, the most oppressive component of burden is the stigma that accompanies a diagnosis of mental illness in our society. Stigma results in the marginalization and ostracism of patients with mental illness; in discrimination in housing, employment, and insurance; in an adverse impact on all aspects of functioning; and in decreased likelihood that they will receive treatment. Often internalized by patients and families, negative social attitudes and expectations may result in a debilitating sense of hopelessness and helplessness, lowered self-esteem, damaged family relationships, and feelings of isolation and shame.[11] One family member observed that the stigma had "translated into an internalized feeling that something is wrong with me"; another wrote of feeling like a "perpetual outsider."

FAMILY RESILIENCE

Because family burden is so well documented, the concept has come to define the family experience of mental illness in many respects. As with any catastrophic stressor, however, mental illness may serve as a catalyst for positive change in families and individuals, an important consideration for practitioners. Namely, the *disintegration* that often accompanies the illness — the breaking down of existing patterns —

offers an opportunity for constructive *reintegration*, as new adaptations and family relationships are forged. In a recent study,[12] my colleagues and I wanted to learn more about the potential for resilience, which is the ability to rebound from adversity and prevail over difficult life circumstances. Our objective was to provide a more balanced picture of the family experience: one that acknowledges strengths as well as limitations, courage as well as despair, and resilience as well as burden.

When our survey participants were asked about any positive family consequences that resulted from the mental illness, most (88%) responded affirmatively. These parents, spouses, siblings, and offspring — and even a few grandparents, aunts, and uncles — told us about their family bonds and commitments, their expanded knowledge and skills, their advocacy activities, and their role in their relative's recovery. In the words of a sibling, "When a family experiences something like this, it makes for very compassionate people — people of substance. My brother has created a bond among us all that we will not allow to be broken." Similarly, a mother proclaimed, "We are proud that our family has remained intact and strong."

We also asked participants whether they as individuals had experienced any positive consequences as a result of the illness. Almost all (99%) reported that they had. One remarked, "I can now say that, like that old aluminum foil ad, I am 'oven-tempered for flexible strength.'" Others mentioned their greater compassion and tolerance, impressive coping skills, healthier attitudes and priorities, contributions as family members and advocates, and greater appreciation of life. In short, their transformative encounter with mental illness has spawned better, stronger, and more caring human beings.

At the same time, it is essential to remember that resilience comes at a terrible price. As one family member expressed it, "Any increased sensitivity to others or any other 'side effects' would be traded in an eyeblink for a healthy relative." Without question, the mental illness of a close relative presents a formidable challenge for families: "I thought that my son's tragedy would completely ruin our lives because it broke our hearts. But we've learned — finally, painfully — not to let this tragedy totally dominate our lives."

Ever mindful of the crushing burden that accosts families, we as practitioners nevertheless need to acknowledge the potential for family resilience under the most challenging circumstances. Moreover, when working with families, we need to encourage and reinforce their constructive adaptation. Many families do manage to prevail over mental illness, creating fulfilling lives in its wake.

FAMILY DIVERSITY

Many variables mediate the impact of mental illness on patients and on family members, including their particular strengths and limitations; their age, gender, and role; and other prior or current problems. Increasingly, professionals are also focusing on the role of cultural diversity and its implications for practice. In contrast to the stance of "cultural blindness" that was favored in the past, current practitioners are encouraged to acknowledge and respect different cultures and to provide culturally sensitive services for patients and families.

Ethnic minorities, including African Americans, Hispanics, Asian Americans, and Native Americans, already comprise an important segment (26.4% in 1995) of the population in the United States and are expected to constitute a majority soon after 2050.[13] Unfortunately, many ethnic minority families find mainstream mental health services alien to their cultural values and traditions. As a result, these families may choose not to seek services, may terminate services prematurely, or may find treatment unhelpful.[14]

Researchers have documented the importance of cultural and ethnic variables in serious mental illness. Deborah Plummer[15] reports that black patients are overrepresented in public psychiatric institutions and more likely than white patients to be committed involuntarily; that low socioeconomic status and minority status jointly influence the quality and degree of services blacks receive; and that individuals who are poor and black often receive temporary services over which their community has no control (and that are eliminated when funds are no longer available). Similarly, Laurene Finley[16] notes that in comparison with nonwhites, whites tend to remain in treatment longer, to obtain more service hours, and to receive residential and social rehabilitation services.

Ethnic and cultural variables also affect the family experience of mental illness. Pertinent issues include differences in family structure, such as the relative importance of the support network (e.g., the "church family"); the central role of the extended family in all aspects of family life; family appraisal of mental illness and its management; barriers to the participation of ethnic minority families in mainstream support groups; and the impact of culture, ethnicity, and social status on caregiving.[17] Increasingly sensitive to these differences, practitioners are designing programs specifically for ethnic minority families.[18] Examples include family network approaches, home-based intervention, long-term linkages with churches and local community groups, and sustained outreach and personal contacts with family members.[19]

FAMILY ADAPTATION

In spite of the oppressive burden that defines the family experience of mental illness, with time most families do learn to cope. They learn about the illness and the service delivery system, acquire the skills needed for effective coping, and develop new sources of social support. As LeRoy Spaniol and Anthony Zipple[20] have observed, families as well as patients can experience recovery. Defining recovery as a process of self-discovery, self-renewal, and transformation, they view this process as marked by specific phases, each with its characteristic dynamics, responses, and tasks.

In fact, when asked directly, most family members say they have moved through a series of phases in coming to terms with the mental illness of their relative.[21] Many professionals have also viewed family adaptation as phase related,[22] although there is no single family pattern or pace of adaptation. Nevertheless, the following phase structure provides a useful framework for understanding family adaptation to serious mental illness.

The Initial Encounter. When first confronted with the mental illness of a close relative, many family members experience feelings of shock, denial, and confusion. Indeed, their initial response is often a paralyzing sense of disbelief. With little understanding of mental illness, family members may dismiss the behavior as a temporary aberration that will disappear with time. Especially during this initial phase, it is important to remember that denial is a common response that may serve a protective function for family members.

Confrontation. Whatever their initial reaction to the onset of their relative's mental illness, eventually family members do come to terms with the illness and its meaning for their lives. The confrontation phase is characterized by intense feelings of grief and loss; a wide range of negative emotions, including anger, guilt, depression, despair, and help-lessness; preoccupation with the illness; and periodic "grief attacks" (acute surges in grief that may interfere with ongoing activities).[23]

Resolution. During the resolution phase, family members experience a gradual decline of the intense feelings experienced earlier. They are able to understand and accept the illness. Although they do not forget the loss, they are able to reinvest their energy in their own lives. They are now able to place the illness in perspective, as a single event in their lives. Some family members become active in advocacy, which can give their life meaning and validity. Often, they join forces with other families through advocacy organizations to work for change in the mental health system and in the larger society.

Posttraumatic Reactions. Although most family members eventually adapt to their altered circumstances, clinicians need to be aware of the potential for posttraumatic reactions, especially among young family members. In my work with adult siblings and offspring,[24] I heard from many family members who manifest the symptoms of posttraumatic stress disorder, including reexperience of the traumatic event (e.g., recurrent painful, intrusive recollections; recurrent dreams or nightmares); diminished responsiveness to the external world (e.g., "psychic numbing"); and a variety of autonomic, dysphoric, or cognitive symptoms (e.g., hyperalertness, sleep disturbance, difficulty concentrating, depression, anxiety).

MEDIATING VARIABLES

A wide range of variables can affect the family adaptation process. Some of these are personal variables, including age, gender, role, personality, physical and mental health, coping effectiveness, values and beliefs, and living arrangements. Family variables can also affect the adaptation process, including composition, social class, ethnic group, religious affiliation, life cycle issues, overall effectiveness, quality of family relationships, and other stressful events confronting the family. Likewise, many social variables can affect family adaptation, including the services available for the patient and family, as well as social values, policies, attitudes, and barriers.

Some of these variables require special consideration, including cultural diversity, which has already been mentioned, and life span issues, which will be addressed later in this book. Three other variables will be discussed here: family effectiveness, family appraisal, and diagnosis.

Family Effectiveness.[25] Like families in general, families of patients with serious mental illness represent a diverse group and vary along a continuum of competence. Some of these families are unusually effective in fulfilling all of their functions and able to cope with the most challenging circumstances. Most families fall someplace in the middle of the continuum, manifesting both strengths and limitations that vary through time and across situations. And some families have difficulty fulfilling even their most basic functions, perhaps because they are struggling with poverty, violence inside or outside the home, addictions, or debilitating health problems. Even the most well-functioning family, however, is likely to be unsettled by the mental illness and its cascading familial aftershocks.[26]

Families typically fulfill certain basic functions: ensuring survival of their members, providing for their safety and security, meeting their emotional and educational needs, coping with crises, advocating for members, and fostering individual and family development. Mental illness often interferes with a family's ability to fulfill some of these functions. Especially at the onset of the illness, for example, families may have few reserves to meet the emotional needs of others, to offer support and companionship, or to engage in recreation and leisure activities. Coping with recurrent illness-related crises, they may also have difficulty performing their educational function: teaching young children social and academic skills, and assisting teenagers with vocational plans.

As the mental illness continues to deplete their resources, families may have difficulty coping with other crises, advocating for individual members, and encouraging their development. At the same time, there are new illness-related tasks: caregiving for the patient with mental illness, coping with the additional stress, and meeting the needs of the now-vulnerable children in the family. Under these circumstances, any preexisting personal, marital, or family problems are likely to be exacerbated.

Family Appraisal.[27] Families may differ significantly in their appraisal of the mental illness, viewing the illness as temporary or permanent, their relative's prospects for recovery as hopeless or hopeful, and their own burden as challenging or crushing. Likewise, families may view themselves as helpless victims or active agents, as effective or ineffective problem solvers, and as a strong or weak family unit. Thus, family adaptation is determined not only by the mental illness, but also by the family's perception of the illness — of its meaning for them — and of their ability to cope with it. Family-focused services can make a significant difference in the family's appraisal, turning helplessness to hopefulness, strengthening beleaguered families, and helping them to recapture their sense of joy and satisfaction.

Diagnosis. The family experience of mental illness varies significantly with different diagnoses. Although there are some universal dimensions of the experience, such as feelings of grief and loss, each diagnosis presents its own challenges. Much of the literature has focused on the family experience of schizophrenia, so I want to mention some of the particular characteristics of mood disorders that determine their impact on families. As David Moltz[28] has discussed, mood disorders, such as bipolar disorder and major depression, have three such characteristics. First, mood disorders are episodic, with a frequent return to the prior level of functioning between episodes. Accordingly, people with these disorders tend to work, to marry, and to have children in spite of their illness. As a result, the patient is often a spouse and parent rather than an adult son or daughter, as is more often the case in schizophrenia.

Second, mood disorders are affective, which also has important consequences for families. As Moltz discusses, affect is "contagious." Namely, interacting with someone who is depressed is an extremely depressing experience. In one study, during their relative's depressive episode, 40% of family members were found to be sufficiently depressed to merit professional attention themselves. This distress was absent between episodes. Similarly, during a manic episode, although the euphoria and elation may be infectious at first, family members are also subject to the irritability and anger that characterize mania.

Third, mood disorders are ambiguous because their symptoms can easily be confused with normal moods. In response to this ambiguity, families may develop inappropriate attitudes about responsibility and self-control. Although patients can often exert some control over early or mild episodes, severe manic episodes are characterized by impairment of judgment, and depressive episodes by paralysis of will. This ambiguity may also cause families to pathologize ordinary manifestations of mood or to respond to normal mood variations with considerable anxiety, fearful that these variations may signal the onset of another episode. Additional confusion may result from the dramatic shifts in personality that often accompany manic and depressive episodes, leaving family members wondering what is "real" and what is a manifestation of the illness.

As Moltz discusses, the episodic, affective, and ambiguous characteristics of mood disorders may have long-term consequences for families. In particular, these features converge in the family's fear of relapse, which may become a preoccupation of patient and family alike. Consequences of this preoccupation may include hypervigilance, constraints on the range of acceptable behavior, a taboo on discussion, and, ultimately, a paralysis that inhibits family growth and development.

FAMILY RISKS

All families are irrevocably changed by the presence of mental illness in their midst. Acting as a sinkhole, the illness depletes the emotional and financial resources of the family and erodes their quality of life. Other time-limited disasters allow family members to replenish their depleted resources, but mental illness is typically woven into the familial fabric on a continuing basis, with the potential for recurrent crises and indefinite expenditures of time, energy, and money. Accosted by a truly seismic event, some families are reconstituted in constructive and adaptive ways. Other families remain together in anguish and disarray, perhaps manifesting entrenched denial or maladaptive coping strategies. Still others disintegrate, their bonds broken beyond repair.

Persistent Denial. Family therapists sometimes use the phrase "the elephant in the living room" to refer to significant problems that cannot be discussed openly. Family members may walk around the "elephant" and ignore its presence, thus preventing painful feelings and conflicts from surfacing. As already noted, denial is a common response at the onset of the illness. When it persists, however, denial keeps families from communicating freely, coping effectively, and offering support to one another. Individuals vary in their coping strategies, pacing, and ultimate degree of acceptance, so a given family may include members with very different degrees of denial.

Families may treat the mental illness as forbidden — or even non-existent — territory for many reasons. Sometimes families internalize the stigma that pervades the larger society and retreat behind a facade of normalcy, fearful that the "family secret" of mental illness will be revealed. They may be poorly informed about the illness, thinking the symptoms are due to a difficult stage or life problem. Families may also be confused about the diagnosis (often with good reason), the most appropriate treatment, and the expected outcome. In response to this confusion — and their own anguish — they may refuse to acknowledge the mental illness or may minimize its seriousness.

Maladaptive Coping Strategies. Although mental illness poses challenges for all families, there are wide differences in their coping effectiveness. Charles Figley[29] specifies 11 characteristics of functional family coping: clear acceptance of the stressor, a family-centered locus of problem, solution-oriented problem solving, high tolerance, clear and direct expressions of commitment and affection, open and effective communication utilization, high family cohesion, flexible family roles, efficient resource utilization, absence of violence, and infrequent substance use. Absence of any of these characteristics is likely to adversely affect the family's ability to cope with mental illness. Some characteristics, such as physical violence or substance abuse, may severely compromise the family's ability to function.

Family Disintegration. Mental illness can assault families with a vengeance, leaving behind a residue of damaged lives and ruptured relationships. Sometimes the assault results in partial or complete disintegration of the family, which can occur in several ways. The patient may be lost to institutional care, to homelessness, or to suicide, leaving behind an eternal void in the family. Well family members, such as a sibling or spouse, may abandon the family in an effort to ensure their own preservation. One woman continues to grieve for her lost childhood, relating that she and her four young siblings were left in the sole care of a mother with mental illness when their father sought a divorce: "When my father left, we were just totally abandoned."

DEVELOPING FAMILY-FOCUSED SERVICES

Given the diversity among families of patients with serious mental illness, an array of interventions are needed that can be tailored to their specific needs, desires, and resources. In this section, I will provide an overview of family services, explore the developmental context of service delivery, and present the Three-Step Model of family intervention.[1] In the next section, I will present five family interventions: family consultation, family support and advocacy groups, family education, family psychoeducation, and psychotherapy. Later in the book, I will discuss the special issues that arise in working with parents, spouses, siblings, and offspring, as well as the implications for intervention.

OVERVIEW OF FAMILY SERVICES

Over the past two decades, family interventions for adults with serious mental illness have proliferated. As Phyllis Solomon[2] has discussed, several factors have stimulated this development. These include (a) the de facto role of families as caregivers who lack the requisite knowledge, skills, and resources; (b) an increasing emphasis on psychosocial interventions that can improve patient quality of life; and (c) research evidence for the effectiveness of family interventions in influencing the course of serious mental illness. Thus, it is an opportune time for practitioners to include these family interventions in their repertoire.

As mentioned earlier, the family interventions to be discussed reflect a historical shift in perspective from the family as a cause of mental illness to the family as a source of support. Acknowledging the supportive role of families, practitioners can assist them in carrying out their caregiving functions, which will in turn promote patient recovery. In fact, most family interventions focus primarily on this caregiving role. Such a focus benefits families along with patients, because improvements in their relative's functioning and quality of life are likely to have a commensurate impact on their own lives.

In addition to their need for effective caregiving, however, families have needs of their own, including their needs to resolve their emotional burden, to preserve the integrity of their own lives, and to fulfill their personal hopes and dreams. Thus, family interventions that focus largely on their supportive role may ignore other important individual and family needs. The overarching goal of professional practice is to assist families in strengthening their family unit and in meeting the needs of all members. Certainly, over the long term, this goal cannot be met by a narrow patient-oriented approach.

Common Features. Although the five family interventions differ in important ways, they have a number of common features.[3] Effective family interventions incorporate the principles of professional practice already discussed, such as approaching families with respect and compassion, applying new competency-based models and collaborative modes, developing an individualized family service plan, and encouraging a sense of hopefulness. Practitioners should also keep abreast of research concerned with serious mental illness and with family interventions. Ultimately, the goal is to assist families in acquiring the knowledge, skills, and resources that will enable them to meet their own needs.

Family interventions are not likely to be effective — or used — unless they address the needs of families themselves. In addition to the family's need for a truly comprehensive and humane system of mental health care, researchers have consistently found that families have three essential needs. First, families need *information* about serious mental illness and its treatment, available community services and resources, and caregiving and management issues. In the words of one family member, "Knowledge has kept me from the depths of hopelessness."

Second, families need *coping skills*, including effective communication, problem-solving, conflict resolution, assertiveness, stress-management, illness management, and relapse prevention skills. Third, families need *support* for themselves. As one family member observed, "The isolation was profound." Potential sources of support for families consist of their informal support network, which includes the nuclear family, the extended family, friends and acquaintances, neighbors, and coworkers; their formal support network, which includes professionals and service providers, social and religious institutions, and the government; and family advocacy groups.

To varying degrees, all effective interventions satisfy these needs. A wide range of services may benefit families, including educational programs, skills-oriented workshops, support groups, and advocacy activities, along with other resources, such as written materials and videotapes. There is solid empirical support for the effectiveness of supportive and educational family interventions.[4] Most services can profit from the involvement of family members as consultants, facilitators, or presenters, either alone or in collaboration with professionals. Involving families in the design, implementation, and evaluation of services increases the likelihood that families will find them responsive to their needs and will choose to participate.

Differences Among Family Interventions. Although they share certain features, effective family interventions also differ in some important respects:

- Relative emphasis on support, information, and skills
- Format, which may involve individual families or multifamily groups
- Inclusion or exclusion of patients
- Mode of facilitation or presentation, which may involve professionals, family members, or a professional-family team
- Setting, which may be the family's home, a mental health agency, or a community organization
- Frequency, duration, and intensity
- Patient phase of illness at the onset of the program
- Family phase of adaptation

Some families may have strong preferences regarding these variations. For instance, a particular family might prefer individual sessions, require home-based services, refuse to participate in long-term interventions, or have special concerns, such as continuity of caregiving among aging parents. An initial consultative session can allow practitioners to respond to family requirements and preferences.[5]

Foci of Intervention. In working with these families, clinicians are likely to be faced with a daunting assortment of issues. At a given time, a family may need assistance in understanding and accepting the illness, in learning about services and community resources, in learning about medication, in developing effective coping skills, in expanding their support network, in providing a supportive environment, or in dealing with family challenges, discussed later in this book, such as treatment nonadherence or substance abuse.

Fortunately, several excellent resources are available to assist both providers and families.[6] Along with my earlier book, *Serious Mental Illness and the Family: The Practitioner's Guide,* useful professional resources include *Schizophrenia: Family Education Methods* by Christopher Amenson; *Helping Families Cope With Mental Illness*, edited by Harriet Lefley and Mona Wasow; the *Teaching Manual for Coping Skills Workshops* by Marilyn Meisel and Edie Mannion; *Bipolar Dis-*

order: A Family-Focused Treatment Approach by David Miklowitz and Michael Goldstein; *Behavioral Family Therapy for Psychiatric Disorders* by Kim Mueser and Shirley Glynn; and *The Role of the Family in Psychiatric Rehabilitation: A Workbook,* edited by LeRoy Spaniol and his colleagues.

Books for patients and family members are also helpful,[7] including *Living Without Depression and Manic Depression: A Workbook for Maintaining Mood Stability* by Mary Ellen Copeland; *Troubled Journey: Coming to Terms With the Mental Illness of a Sibling or Parent,* which I wrote with Rex Dickens; *Bipolar Disorder: A Guide for Patients and Families* by Francis Mondimore; *Coping With Schizophrenia: A Guide for Families* by Kim Mueser and Susan Gingerich; *Overcoming Depression* by Demitri Papolos and Janice Papolos; *Surviving Schizophrenia: A Manual for Families, Consumers and Providers* by E. Fuller Torrey; *The Skipping Stone: Ripple Effects of Mental Illness on the Family* by Mona Wasow; and *When Someone You Love Has a Mental Illness* by Rebecca Woolis.

Another essential resource is family advocacy organizations, such as NAMI (formerly the National Alliance for the Mentally Ill), which has over a thousand state and local affiliates throughout the country. As I was writing this section, I heard from a father in Pennsylvania whose adult son — off medication and very psychotic — was missing in California. I referred the distraught father to the NAMI California affiliate, which helped him locate his son in Los Angeles and obtain urgently needed hospitalization. Other helpful advocacy organizations are the National Depressive and Manic Depressive Association (NDMDA) and the National Mental Health Association.

The Intervention Process. Applying the principles of adult education, Amenson[8] points out that families have a variety of learning styles and often require time and practice to master the necessary skills. Using a cooking analogy, he encourages practitioners to provide a balanced diet of consultation, support, education, skill building, and therapy, mixing these ingredients in creative ways to match an endless variety of circumstances. Amenson reminds practitioners that mental illness creates tremendous family stress, which in turn can impede new learning. Providers need to provide a supportive environment in which families can relinquish or modify their unsuccessful coping efforts and develop more effective skills and strategies.

In addition to the differences among family interventions, professionals also need to respond to the differences among families, including their developmental agenda.

THE DEVELOPMENTAL CONTEXT

Life span development provides an essential context for professional practice with families.[9] Over time, as John Rolland[10] has discussed, changes occur in individual family members, in the family system, and in the illness itself. In turn, these changes affect the family's response to mental illness, the needs of family members, and the services that can address those needs. Given the diversity among individuals, families, and illnesses, any discussion of their life cycles must proceed with some caution. Normative phases and tasks may not apply to all individuals or to all families, and each illness has its own character and poses its particular challenges. Nevertheless, individuals, families, and illnesses all change with time; and these changes are an important consideration in professional practice.

A developmental context is important for two reasons. First, the needs and concerns of family members change with their altered circumstances. Consider the case of parents who have an adult son with schizophrenia. At the time of their son's initial hospitalization, these parents are serving as primary caregivers who have urgent needs for information about mental illness and available services, for practical coping skills, and for support for themselves. With effective treatment, their son begins to recover and regain control of his life. His parents may need assistance in supporting their son's treatment and recovery, in dealing with specific illness-related problems, or in fulfilling personal or marital goals under altered circumstances. Still later, these now-aging parents are concerned about continuity of caregiving for their son, who works part time at a consumer-run drop-in center but still resides at home. At this juncture, the parents request information about community housing, disability benefits, and estate planning. Their changing agenda requires an evolving family service plan.

Second, the impact of mental illness on family members depends partly on its timing in their life span and on their particular role within the family. As a result, individual family members have special experiences, needs, and concerns in their role as parent, spouse, sibling, or offspring. Their personal legacy reflects the specific developmental tasks that were disrupted as a result of the illness, leaving a residue of "unfinished business" in their wake. In understanding the consequences of mental illness for family members, it is vital to pose Rolland's[11] essential developmental questions: What life plans have the family or individual members had to cancel, postpone, or alter? Whose plans are most and least affected?

As these questions suggest, children and adolescents — the siblings and offspring of patients with mental illness — share a special vulnerability to the disruptive force of mental illness. Young family members are more easily overwhelmed than adults by stressful events. They have fewer coping skills and psychological defenses, as well as more limited ability to understand the illness and to verbalize painful feelings. Furthermore, children are more dependent on other people in their lives, a precarious position when a parent or older sibling suffers from mental illness. Equally important, because young family members are still developing, the illness is woven into their very sense of self, becoming *part* of them rather than something that merely happens to their family.

Because of their common developmental context, young siblings and offspring also share an array of illness-related risks and concerns, both as children and as adults. Sometimes they share both roles as well; 25% of our survey participants reported they were both siblings and offspring.[12] Among their risks as first-degree relatives, these family members experience an increased risk of developing mental illness themselves.[13] In contrast to a 1% incidence of schizophrenia in the general population, the risk of developing the disorder has been estimated at 9% for siblings and 13% for offspring. The risk of developing bipolar disorder among first-degree relatives is about 1 in 12 (8%). This risk increases when the family includes more than one person with mental illness.

As researchers have documented in numerous studies,[14] young family members are also subject to a range of cognitive, social, emotional, behavioral, academic, and developmental problems. For example, in our survey, at least three-quarters of adult siblings and offspring reported the following illness-related concerns: caregiving for their relative (94%); family disruption (83%); difficulty balancing personal and family needs (81%); a belief that their own needs had not been met (79%); feelings of helplessness and hopelessness (75%); and poor self-esteem (75%).

In spite of these risks, it is equally clear that many variables mediate the risks for particular siblings and offspring, who remain a diverse group throughout their lives. In reality, many do very well under challenging circumstances:

My husband once asked me how it was possible that I evolved unscathed from my upbringing with a mentally ill brother. It never occurred to me that as a family we should have fallen apart. To me my brother's illness was just a fact, like Daddy went to work on Monday mornings. It was okay for him to be that way, and it was okay for us to be happy. It was simple — you love your family, you care for each individual, you respect each other. It always felt solid, it felt right.

In fact, when asked in our survey if they had experienced any positive consequences as a result of the mental illness in their families, a large majority (86%) of adult siblings and offspring answered affirmatively. Namely, they had become better human beings: stronger, more compassionate, and more competent. As noted earlier, however, resilience often exacts a high personal price and follows an exceedingly troubled journey: "I became the perfect child to spare my parents more grief. But I have spent my life trying to run away from this problem. Feeling guilty and helpless, the unending sorrow for not being able to help."

The Individual Life Cycle. Depending upon its timing, the mental illness might undermine the acquisition of basic trust during infancy, the development of peer relationships and academic skills during childhood, and the establishment of a secure sense of identity during adolescence. A child who is confronted from birth with the illness of a primary caregiver may be vulnerable to all of these risks. A family member recalled being unable to concentrate in school because all of her energy was "directed toward what was happening at home and what was going to become of our family."

A young adult sibling may have difficulty with separation, intimacy, and vocational plans. In the words of one sibling, "I was trying to find my place in the world, and my brother disrupted this world." Another sibling — who grew up with a brother and sister who both had schizophrenia — spoke of his legacy: "As an adult, I've found intimacy and sexual relationships extremely difficult. I'm afraid of having children."

Parents of an adult child with mental illness are also likely to find that their caregiving role sometimes preempts their developmental agenda. The launching of children into the adult world, which is the main task of family life, may never be completed. Adult-to-adult relationships with grown children may never be realized. Parents may long for an "empty nest" that never arrives, and for the freedom that is expected to characterize middle and late adulthood. In the words of one midlife mother, "You're just not free. The biggest problem is the prison that it puts us in." Later in life, aging parents may again find their developmental agenda erased by a more important consideration: continuity of caregiving for their adult child with mental illness.

The following table[15] of developmental phases and tasks offers a useful framework for working with family members over time.

TABLE 3: DEVELOPMENTAL PHASES AND TASKS*

Infancy:	Survival
	Attachment
	Basic trust
Preschool Period:	Socialization
	Cognitive development
	Social development
	Emotional development
	Behavioral development
	Identification
	Gender identity
	Self-concept
Middle Childhood:	Academic adjustment
	Peer relations
Adolescence:	Identity
	Sexuality
	Career plans
	Separation
Young Adulthood:	Intimacy
	Marriage/Partnership
	Parenthood
	Vocational commitment
Middle Adulthood:	Renegotiation of commitments
	Launching of children
Late Adulthood:	Retirement
	Financial security
	Loss of intimate relationships
	Personal illness and mortality
	Life review
	Grandparenthood

---

*__Note__. Adapted from *Serious Mental Illness and the Family: The Practitioner's Guide* (p. 81), by D. T. Marsh, 1998, New York: Wiley. Copyright 1998 by John Wiley & Sons, Inc. Reprinted by permission of John Wiley & Sons, Inc.

The Family Life Cycle. Individual development takes place largely within the family, however defined. As we are regularly informed by a barrage of statistics, the traditional nuclear family — breadwinning father, homemaker mother, and children — is no longer the most common family system. Other family structures have become more prevalent, including ethnic minority, two-career, single-parent, teenage, cohabiting, blended, and gay and lesbian families. Gender roles and relationships have also been changing, with males and females more likely to share financial and caregiving responsibilities.

The following family life cycle is reasonably appropriate for most families that include children. In specifying the following successive phases and tasks, Betty Carter and Monica McGoldrick[16] provide a framework for understanding the potential impact on a member's mental illness on family growth and development. They have described six phases in the family life cycle:

- Launching of the single young adult from the family of origin
- Joining of families through marriage
- Becoming parents and adjusting to young children
- Transforming the family system in adolescence
- Launching children and moving on
- Changing in later life

As with the individual life cycle, all of these phases and their associated tasks may be disrupted by the presence of mental illness.

An additional risk, as Rolland[17] discusses, is that chronic illness may intensify family cohesion, ultimately freezing the family into a permanent state of fusion and fixation on the illness. Such a narrow familial focus may undermine the autonomy of individual family members, foreclose opportunities outside the family, and undermine other family relationships, including marital, parent-child, and sibling relationships. In the words of one sibling, "I lost out on my childhood. Most of my memories include a sickly older sister who got all of the attention by having repeated crises."

The Mental Illness Life Cycle. Along with the life cycles of the individual and the family, the mental illness life cycle has a major impact on the life plans and tasks of family members. Rolland specifies four dimensions of illness, each of which is assumed to have an impact on the family: onset, course, outcome, and incapacitation. Onset of illness represents a continuum that ranges from acute to chronic. The onset of serious mental illness may be either sudden or gradual, as may subsequent episodes. Sudden onset confronts the family with pressing demands for adaptation, whereas gradual onset may pose problems for families who fail to recognize the emergence of the illness.

Course of illness may be progressive, constant, or relapsing/episodic. Over time, serious mental illness may manifest all of these patterns. In response, families may struggle to cope with an illness that is continually symptomatic, that results in some relatively stable deficits, and that alternates between periods of remission and exacerbation. Opportunities for respite may be minimal, and there are inherent risks of exhaustion and hypervigilance for primary caregivers.

With respect to outcome, patients with serious mental illness have the potential for full recovery, partial recovery, or no recovery. As a result, the family — including the patient — may remain in a kind of prognostic limbo, hoping for recovery but fearing recurrence. The final dimension is incapacitation, which includes both actual impairment and social stigma. Although there is substantial individual variability, serious mental illness inherently involves significant functional limitations. Likewise, stigma is universally associated with mental illness in our society; indeed, the stigma is often experienced as a greater burden than the illness itself.

THE THREE-STEP MODEL[18]

The following model can assist practitioners in achieving an optimal service match for particular families and settings. Incorporating the material already presented, the model encourages a competency-based and collaborative mode of working with families, as well as an individualized approach to family services, because there is no way to know in advance which services will be most helpful for a given family at a particular time. The model includes three sequential steps: (a) offering an initial family consultation session; (b) assisting families to select and access a combination of consultative, educational, skills-oriented, and supportive services; and (c) recommending psychotherapy for those families who continue to experience significant problems. Specific family interventions and their implementation will be discussed later in this book.

Step 1. At the onset of the illness, family consultation offers a useful means of engaging families and of assisting them to identify and prioritize their needs, to deal with illness-related concerns, to make an informed choice about their use of other available services, and to formulate a family service plan. Consultation may be sufficient for some families, especially if it is offered at the time of the initial diagnosis and thereafter as needed, such as during crises, periods of inpatient treatment, and life span transitions.

Step 2. Families of patients with serious mental illness share certain essential needs, including their needs for information, skills, and support. In a given community, a variety of resources may help families address these needs, including the local NAMI affiliate, which may offer a family support group and a variety of educational programs. Professional services may also be helpful, such as consultative sessions on an as-needed basis, a provider-based support group, educational or skills-oriented workshops, or a more intensive psychoeducational program. When integrated into an individualized family service plan, Steps 1 and 2 are likely to meet the needs of most families.

Step 3. Family members who continue to experience significant problems may be appropriate candidates for individual, couple, or family therapy, either singly or in combination. Individual therapy can assist family members to resolve issues of grief, loss, guilt, and responsibility. Couple therapy can help marital partners manage illness-related conflicts and other relational problems. Family therapy can foster improvements in communication, problem-solving, conflict resolution, and symptom management skills. Group therapy may reduce feelings of isolation and allow families to share their stories and coping strategies.

Implementing the Model. The Three-Step Model simply offers a general structure than can be adapted to meet the needs of specific practitioners, families, and settings. In implementing the model, providers may be constrained by professional and community resources; the needs of particular patients and families; the requirements of solo, group, or agency-based practice; and the mandates of behavioral health care programs, which typically emphasize time-limited, efficient, and cost-effective interventions. In working with families, clinicians should also be sensitive to the ethical and legal context of professional practice, which will be discussed later in this book.

Regardless of the potential value of family interventions, some families may decline all services or may terminate their participation prematurely. Requesting feedback from families, practitioners can gain insight into their reasons for declining or terminating services, which may include lack of time or insurance coverage, alienation from the mental health system, family disengagement, or various personal, family, or cultural considerations. Such feedback can assist professionals to tailor service plans for individual families and to develop more satisfactory and responsive family-focused services.

FAMILY INTERVENTIONS

This section presents five effective family interventions: family consultation, family support and advocacy groups, family education, family psychoeducation, and psychotherapy. All have potential value and can be modified to meet the requirements of particular providers, families, and settings.[1] I will describe each of these interventions in an order that reflects the Three-Step Model presented previously.

FAMILY CONSULTATION

Family consultation offers a useful intervention in the area of serious mental illness.[2] At the onset of the illness, consultation provides a means of engaging families and assisting them to identify and prioritize their needs. During an initial consultative session, practitioners can help families deal with illness-related concerns, make an informed choice about their use of other available services, and formulate a family service plan. Consultation may be sufficient for some families, especially if it is offered at the point of initial diagnosis and thereafter on an as-needed basis, such as during crises or periods of inpatient treatment.

As practiced by mental health professionals, family consultation has much in common with the consultative services offered by other professionals, such as accountants and attorneys. In each case, consultants offer expert knowledge, skills, and advice to families, who maintain primary responsibility for determining their own goals, for deciding whether to accept professional recommendations, and for implementing decisions. Family satisfaction is a central outcome variable in consultation, along with increased family competence and confidence.

A consultative approach fosters collaborative relationships with families, provides an objective and systems-oriented assessment of their concerns, emphasizes family strengths and resources, and facilitates the shift to alternative professional roles as appropriate. Consultative sessions may have many foci, such as helping the family to cope with symptomatic behavior, to make decisions about living arrangements, to deal with a concurrent substance abuse disorder, or to undertake long-term planning.

Practitioners should distinguish between consultation and psycho-therapy in working with families and make sure the distinction is clear to family members. In fact, the central difference between the two fam-ily interventions is captured in their dictionary definitions. Consulta-tion is defined as asking the advice or opinion of an expert and as delib-erating together, whereas therapy involves the treatment of mental or emotional disorders by psychological means. In professional practice, of course, there is some overlap between the two interventions, and a particular family may present with both consultative and therapeutic issues. Nevertheless, there are important distinctions between these approaches,[3] as indicated in the table on page 47.

Psychologist June Husted[4] has many years of experience as both a clinician/administrator at a Department of Veterans Affairs medical center and an independent practitioner. Based on her experience with both agency-based and independent family consultation, she considers the former to be far more effective. Involvement with both patients and families increases the information available to staff and provides a more thorough picture of the patient's history and illness and of the family's needs and concerns. As well, information from the family can be incor-porated into the treatment plan, such as problems with treatment adher-ence, family stressors that affect the patient, or unacceptable behaviors that might benefit from intervention.

The needs of families themselves can also be addressed. Illustrat-ing her work as an agency-based consultant, Husted shares the follow-ing encounter:

> The parents came into my office with frustrated, angry looks
> on their faces, escorting their decompensating son. "It's been
> hell living with him these past 20 years," his mother exclaimed,
> as if it were his fault. I acknowledged how horrible it is for the
> patient and the family to live with this brain disorder and edu-

TABLE 4: DIFFERENCES BETWEEN FAMILY CONSULTATION AND FAMILY THERAPY*

Family Consultation		Family Therapy
	Paradigm	
Family competence		Family dysfunction
	Professional Role	
Consultant		Therapist
	Family Role	
Consultee		Client
	Mode	
Collaborative		Authoritarian
	Focus of Intervention	
Family agenda		Family system
	Goal	
Enhanced family coping		Reduced family dysfunction
	Outcome Measure	
Family satisfaction		Patient improvement
	Communication	
Open, direct, and complete		Often partially concealed
	Family Status	
Part of patient's treatment team		Part of patient's treatment plan
	Family Service Plan	
One component of service plan		Often sole family service

*Note. Adapted from *Serious Mental Illness and the Family: The Practitioner's Guide* (p. 139), by D. T. Marsh, 1998, New York: Wiley. Copyright 1998 by John Wiley & Sons, Inc. Reprinted by permission of John Wiley & Sons, Inc.

cated them about schizophrenia. The mother looked stunned by the realization that many of his behaviors were symptoms of the illness, not volitional behaviors. The change in the family's response to him, as well as a modification of his medication suggested by their description of the pattern of his illness, had a major impact on his improvement. In later months, I learned that their family relationships had improved significantly and that their son was now included in family dinners and celebrations.

Husted notes that an independent practitioner may see a family member under two different circumstances: for personal problems that may be affected by the illness or for patient-related crises or problems. She offers the following example:

> I met several times with a family in which the father had a difficult time accepting his son's schizophrenia and was constantly pressuring the son to do more to obtain regular employment. I educated the family about the limitations that resulted from the illness, taught the father some ways he could positively reinforce his son's efforts and progress, and resolved some areas of family conflict. There was no feedback on the resolution of these issues, but a year later I was pleased to see the family participating in a special reception for a job program for people with serious mental illness. The son was a successful participant.

FAMILY SUPPORT AND ADVOCACY GROUPS

National mental health advocacy organizations serve as a major resource for families. Most families are likely to benefit from a referral to NAMI, which has over a thousand local affiliates in all 50 states. A referral to other groups may also be helpful, such as the National Depressive and Manic Depressive Association (NDMDA). Practitioners can encourage families to join local support and advocacy groups, explain the benefits of participation, and provide telephone contact numbers. Family members consistently attest to the value of such groups: "The group has been like a beacon, providing me with information, support, and understanding."

Family support and advocacy groups serve three important functions. First, these groups provide vital support through member-facilitated support groups and informal networking. Second, they offer a variety of educational programs through local affiliates and at state and national conventions. Many local NAMI affiliates offer the Family-to-Family Education Program, a 12-week educational program presented by trained family members. Third, these groups encourage advocacy, as members join forces to work for expanded research and improved services throughout the country.

Contacts between professionals and advocacy groups can be mutually beneficial. Most groups welcome presentations by practitioners at their monthly meetings. In turn, providers will gain insight into family experiences and concerns, and families will feel comfortable contacting them when needed. Clinicians can also benefit from attending NAMI conventions, where they will gain knowledge about serious mental illness, innovative treatments, and effective coping strategies. This knowledge is essential for practitioners who use any of the family interventions described in this section.

FAMILY EDUCATION

Families have a pressing need for information about mental illness and its treatment, about caregiving and management issues, about the mental health system and community resources, and about family coping and adaptation. Professionals can meet this need by offering a variety of educational programs, typically ranging from a 1-day workshop to a 10- or 12-week series. The following topics are generally covered: serious mental illness and its treatment; community resources; family experiences and needs; coping strategies and skills; and specific problems, such as symptom management. Most programs also offer an opportunity for family members to ask questions and to network with other families. Several excellent resources are available that describe educational programs.[5]

Numerous studies have shown the value of family education.[6] Benefits for families include

- increased understanding and acceptance of mental illness;
- more realistic expectations and improved family relationships;
- enhanced coping effectiveness;
- reduced stigma and isolation; and
- a greater sense of hopefulness.

Benefits for patients include

- a more constructive family environment;
- increased knowledge of community services and resources;
- family support for the treatment and rehabilitation plan;
- reduced risk of relapse; and
- improvements in the mental health system.

As one family member observed, "Family education enabled us to be a help rather than a hindrance."

The following 10-week educational program (Table 5) is appropriate for families that have relatives with schizophrenia or a mood disorder.[7] The format can be modified to meet the requirements of different providers, settings, and diagnostic groups. Weekly 90-minute sessions can include a mix of didactic material, videotapes, and handouts, as well as an opportunity for social interaction.

TABLE 5: 10-WEEK FAMILY EDUCATION PROGRAM*

Week 1. Nature and Purpose of Program
Introductions, overview of program, survey of family members

Week 2. Family-Professional Relationships
Collaboration, roles and responsibilities, channels of communication

Week 3. Mental Illness I
Schizophrenia: etiology, symptoms, treatment, prognosis

Week 4. Mental Illness II
Mood disorders: etiology, symptoms, treatment, prognosis

Week 5. The Family Experience
Family burden and needs, life span perspectives, family roles

Week 6. Stress, Coping, and Adaptation
Family adaptation, coping resources, and strategies

Week 7. Enhancing Personal and Family Effectiveness I
Communication, problem solving, conflict resolution, stress management

Week 8. Enhancing Personal and Family Effectiveness II
Assertiveness, self-care, illness management, relapse prevention

Week 9: Dealing With Specific Problems
Symptoms, setting limits, substance abuse, other concerns

Week 10. A Comprehensive System of Community-Based Care
Services, providers, and resources; family support; referrals

***Note**. Adapted from *Serious Mental Illness and the Family: The Practitioner's Guide* (p. 165), by D. T. Marsh, 1998, New York: Wiley. Copyright 1998 by John Wiley & Sons, Inc. Reprinted by permission of John Wiley & Sons, Inc.

FAMILY PSYCHOEDUCATION

Although the terms *education* and *psychoeducation* are sometimes used interchangeably, there are important differences between the two interventions. Educational programs are primarily designed to address the need of families for information about mental illness and family concerns. Family psychoeducation includes education but goes beyond, with the objective of enhancing the family's ability to cope with the serious mental illness and to reduce the patient's risk of relapse.

Psychoeducational programs generally include both patient and family interventions. Patient components consist of education about mental illness and its management, emphasis on medication adherence, and training in social skills. Family components typically involve (a) an empathic, validating, nonblaming, task-oriented alliance with the family; (b) education about mental illness and its management; (c) training in coping skills, such as communication, problem solving, and stress management; and (d) social support, especially through contact with other families.

As is the case for pharmacological treatment, there is growing evidence that a minimum amount of psychoeducational treatment is required to obtain maximum benefits. Interventions of at least 9 months may be necessary to see effects, although some psychoeducational interventions continue for a year or more.[8] There is strong evidence that psychoeducation reduces the rate of patient relapse, as well as suggestive evidence that this intervention improves patient functioning and family well-being. There is also persuasive evidence that education alone is less effective than interventions that provide support, problem solving, and crisis intervention, and that dynamic approaches are ineffective.

The advantages of family psychoeducation argue for its availability for all families who are involved with their relatives. Namely, this intervention encourages family-professional collaboration, meets many family needs, and has strong empirical support. Certainly, psychoeducation is the preferred strategy for reducing the risk of patient relapse. On the other hand, this intervention is primarily offered by a professional team over a relatively long period, which may limit psychoeducation to certain practitioners, families, and settings.

There is increasing interest in family psychoeducation, which can be provided to individual families or multifamily groups.[9] In their book *Behavioral Family Therapy for Psychiatric Disorders,* Kim Mueser and Shirley Glynn[10] provide a wealth of practical information for practitioners who work with families. The Behavioral Family Therapy (BFT) model includes six components: (a) engagement (1-3 sessions); (b) assessment (1-3 sessions with each individual; follow-up individual and family sessions every 3-4 months); (c) education (2-4 sessions); (d) communication skills training (if needed, 4-10 sessions); (e) problem-solving training (4-12 sessions); and (f) special problems, such as substance abuse (1-5 sessions).

Bipolar Disorder: A Family-Focused Treatment Approach by David Miklowitz and Michael Goldstein[11] is similarly useful for practitioners who wish to offer family psychoeducation in mood disorders.

COUNSELING OR PSYCHOTHERAPY

The family interventions discussed so far primarily offer education, skills training, and support. These are the initial interventions of choice for most families. If these interventions are not sufficient, however, other services may also be appropriate, including counseling or psychotherapy, which may vary in format (individual, couple, family, or group); in strategies and techniques; and in duration, frequency, and intensity. The distinction is sometimes made between counseling, which refers to briefer, less intensive, and more supportive forms of treatment, and psychotherapy, which is appropriate for severe and deep-seated problems.

Individual counseling or psychotherapy may be beneficial for family members who prefer the privacy and intimacy of a confidential therapeutic relationship or are having difficulty resolving issues of grief, loss, guilt, and responsibility. Some siblings and offspring appear to be appropriate candidates for individual therapy. In my research,[12] 75% of adult siblings and offspring reported they had sought personal therapy; 90% of those who were under age 10 at the onset of their relative's illness had sought therapy, as had an identical percentage of those who were both siblings and offspring. Almost all reported therapy was very helpful.

Couple therapy can assist partners to resolve illness-related conflicts and other relational problems. During couple therapy precipitated by a marital crisis, a sibling discovered that her current problems were related to her family history: "My sister's schizophrenia had deeply affected me, and I'd never consciously realized it. This crisis in our life was a new beginning for us. We began to reconstruct our marriage." Likewise, family therapy may be helpful when there are preexisting problems in communication or conflict management, the family is unable to cope adequately with their relative's mental illness, or success-ful treatment of an individual requires the involvement of other family members.

Both couple and family therapy carry potential risks, including de-flection from personal problems and concerns in couple therapy, and loss of privacy and increased family disruption in family therapy. Ad-ditional risks are associated with general prescriptions of family therapy that are based on unsupported assumptions of family dysfunction or pathogenesis or that do not take into account the needs and desires of particular families.

In spite of these risks, psychotherapy can have a life-enhancing impact on family members. Here are the words of a mother:

> More than a decade after my son was diagnosed with mental illness, I would say that my personal therapy was a major fac-tor in my own recovery. During the most difficult period of my life, I found a sanctuary in therapy: a place to grieve, to express my anger and frustration, to somehow find the strength to get through each day. I will be forever grateful to my therapist, who helped me recapture my passion for life.

Especially for siblings and offspring, therapy can offer an opportu-nity to explore "the principle of the past in the present"[13] — to come to terms with the phantoms that move across the stage of memory — and to learn what Al-Anon has termed "detaching with love." Here are the words of an adult sibling:

> I was so depressed and lonely. I even thought of suicide. For many years, I looked for answers to my brother's problems, never realizing I had to find myself first. I have — being in therapy, learning I'm okay. I am what I want to be — a caring, nurturing person.

WORKING WITH INDIVIDUAL
FAMILY MEMBERS

Although there are universal dimensions to the family experience of mental illness, many variables mediate the impact on individual family members, including their age, gender, and role in the family. Accordingly, the unique concerns of parents, spouses, siblings, and offspring merit the attention of practitioners. In this section, I will explore each of the family roles, with emphasis on their implications for professional practice.[1]

PARENTS

Compared with other members of the family, parents — especially mothers — have had the most contact with researchers and clinicians. Thus, there is greater understanding of parents and of the interventions that can address their needs. In fact, much of the material covered thus far in the book depicts the parental experience of mental illness. Nevertheless, several parental themes merit special attention, including grief and loss, primary caregiving, guilt and responsibility, intrusions into the family life space, and marital stress.

Parents typically experience a range of intense losses, both real and symbolic, when a child of any age develops serious mental illness. They may mourn for the loss of the well child for whom there was so much potential, for the loss of their normal family, and for the loss of their own hopes and dreams. One mother lamented, "The sense of what might have been is overwhelming"; another tearfully recalled, "The problems with my daughter were like a black hole inside of me into which everything else had been drawn."

Parents are most likely to assume roles as primary caregivers or informal case managers, sometimes for a lifetime.[2] At any time, they may hear the call to caregiving, which may become the central motif in their lives. Mothers often pay a high price for their caregiving role, sometimes tabling their own agenda in the process. As they grow older, parents express a universal concern about continuity of caregiving, wondering who will take over the caregiving after they are gone.

In addition, parents are prone to feelings of guilt and responsibility, which may be intensified by professionals who espouse earlier conceptual models of family pathogenesis or dysfunction. Their feelings of responsibility partly reflect the cultural edict: If there is a troubled child, there must be troubling parents. Internalized by mothers, this edict adds significantly to their burden. Parents are also likely to complain about intrusions into the family life space. Repeatedly accosted by well-intentioned professionals who are trying to help their child, parents may feel their family has lost both its privacy and its integrity. At the same time, the stress and disruption accompanying the illness create fertile ground for marital conflict,[3] especially at the onset of the illness. One mother declared, "My daughter has ripped our family apart, ripped us apart, given us so much grief."

Recent research findings[4] suggest that mothers and fathers may respond to their shared tragedy in very different ways. For decades, behavioral scientists have assumed that human beings respond to severe stress with a "fight or flight" response in which their body prepares for either aggression or hasty withdrawal. In fact, that response now appears to be characteristic only of males. When faced with stress, females are more prone to "tend and befriend" as they strive to protect and nurture their children and to reach out to supportive females. Thus, just as mothers are becoming enmeshed in the vortex of caregiving and turning to others, fathers may be taking flight from clamorous family demands and unmanageable emotions.

Whatever the eventual outcome, the marriage contract is inevitably renegotiated as a result of a child's mental illness. Sometimes the illness becomes forbidden territory — the "elephant in the living room" mentioned earlier. Sometimes the marriage does not endure. And sometimes the marriage is reconstructed in fulfilling ways: "We've been married over 30 years. I think it's made our marriage stronger because we've shared the grief and we've shared the joys."

SPOUSES

The discussion in this section refers specifically to spouses, although others may also seek professional services to cope with the mental illness of someone with whom they share a long-term commitment. Given the challenges that accompany mental illness, however, practitioners are most likely to be working with spouses. For ease of communication, I use the term *spouse* to refer to the well husband or wife, as well as other life companions, and the term *partner* to refer to the person with serious mental illness.

At least half a million people with serious mental illness are assumed to reside with a husband or wife, and the actual figure may be considerably higher.[5] An estimated 30% to 35% of hospitalized patients are discharged to live with their spouses. The burden of these family members is substantial: "My husband's schizophrenia is like a third member in our marriage. It is always there. Even with medication, we still deal with his paranoia, his isolation, and his need for my full attention on a daily basis."[6] Yet spouses have received relatively little attention in the professional literature or, in fact, from professionals themselves.[7] In the words of one angry spouse, "They see us as the enemy."

Important spousal themes include grief and loss, marital problems, difficult choices, "single parenting," and financial distress. Spouses typically experience a range of emotional, social, and economic losses similar to those that accompany spousal bereavement, often feeling that they are no longer married to the same person. They typically assume increased responsibility for parenting and other aspects of family life, struggle to manage full-time employment and household responsibilities, and face continuing disruption and stress. Many spouses must shoulder this burden without much assistance from their partner. Exhaustion and burnout are virtually inevitable, at least occasionally and sometimes unremittingly. Often, they fight a losing battle to balance their own needs with those of other family members: "A spouse gets totally LOST in the wants and needs of the ill partner."

Marital problems are inevitable when a partner has mental illness. Researchers[8] have documented a range of illness-related problems, including marital dissatisfaction and disruption, the failure of partners to assume responsibility for the illness, an absence of reciprocity, symptomatic behavior, role distortions, impaired sexual relations, and the need to set limits. In one study, 50% of spouses married to partners with major mood disorders reported they would not have married if they had known more about the illness; a similar proportion had seriously considered separation or divorce. Virtually all research findings point to spousal feelings of frustration, isolation, exhaustion, and depression.

Even when they find the marriage intolerable, spouses may feel they face only difficult choices and, especially if there are children, no good choices at all.[9] On one hand, they may find themselves bound to a relationship that drains their emotional and financial resources. On the other hand, spouses have made a commitment to someone they have vowed to love, honor, and cherish in sickness and in health. Under these circumstances, they are likely to experience substantial conflict and guilt if they consider separation or divorce. If they do remain in the marriage, spouses may feel they have become "single parents." One woman complained that she was "doing the roles of mother, wife, and father." As well, spouses typically worry about the genetic and psycho-social risks for their children.

The mental illness of a partner, especially a primary wage earner, frequently compromises the economic security of the family. As one spouse has pointed out,[10] a partner's mental illness may result in job loss, a leave of absence, loss of opportunities for advancement, reduced benefits for retirement, and loss of insurance coverage and other benefits. Symptom-related problems, such as the spending sprees associated with bipolar disorder, may further deplete the family's resources. These financial problems are compounded by the ineligibility of married individuals with mental disabilities for some benefits available to those who are single.

Although the spousal burden is often oppressive, it is important to recognize that some couples do not experience this level of marital distress. Like all long-term relationships, the intricate tapestry of these marriages is woven of various threads comprising memories, rituals, celebrations, joys, and sorrows. In describing her husband, one wife observed that he brings much to their marriage and their family life: "Despite his illness, he is a source of strength, comfort, and support. We are learning together how to accommodate to the illness and to minimize its intrusion into our lives."

SIBLINGS

More than 80% of children in the United States are siblings — brothers and sisters who share a very special bond.[11] Our siblings know us like no one else, spend more time with us than other family members, strongly influence our personality and relationships, meet important needs for us, influence us throughout our lives, and are partners in our longest relationship.[12] When one sibling develops a mental illness, it has a profound impact on this relationship. Important sibling themes include grief and loss, a sense of being forgotten family members, sibling survivor's guilt, the "replacement child syndrome,"[13] and the personal legacy.

Siblings may mourn for their well brother or sister, for a shared past now shadowed by a painful present, and for the loss of an anticipated future with a healthy relative. As one sibling expressed it, "To me, it was a death. The person whom I knew and was so much like me in so many ways had died, and I didn't know this person who was living in the house any more."[14] Unlike a biological death, however, siblings need to adapt to an altered relationship, which can be surpassingly difficult: "I have found it almost impossible to let go of what our relationship once was and accept what our relationship has become."[15]

The sense of being forgotten family members reverberates through the personal accounts of siblings. When their sister developed mental illness, one of two siblings wrote, "My brother and I felt there was no time for us; everyone was consumed by what was going on with my sister. We no longer mattered."[16] Outside of the family, siblings are ignored by a mental health system that seems impervious to their distress and concerns.

Survivor's guilt is experienced by siblings simply because they have been spared mental illness themselves. Through the fault of neither, one sibling has remained well; the other suffers from mental illness. The unfairness of this reality is likely to color the lives of well siblings, who may shoulder an irrational belief that somehow their own health has been achieved at the expense of their brother or sister. Under these circumstances, they may find their life stripped of pleasure by the illness. At the same time, siblings may place themselves in the role of a "replacement child" who can compensate their devastated parents. Striving to be perfect children, they may deny themselves opportunities for healthy rebellion.

Their encounter with mental illness results in a personal legacy among well siblings that permeates all aspects of their lives: their feelings about themselves, their academic and vocational lives, and their relationships inside and outside the family. One sibling said that her sister's mental illness had translated into "a pervasive sense of shame"; another remarked, "The pain and grief made it impossible for me to enjoy the 'best years' of my life."

Growing up, siblings may feel alienated from peers: "I felt unacceptable to my peers and restricted my friendships to a few people who accepted me and did not ask too many questions." As adults — now painfully aware of the risks that accompany our most intimate relationships — they may have difficulty trusting others or making a long-term commitment. If they do marry, siblings may worry about the risk of mental illness in their own children and struggle to balance their commitments to their two families: "I worry about the present and future."

At the same time, well siblings may also enjoy the gratifications that can accompany our longest relationship. One woman recalled a difficult adolescence marked by a sense that her "point of reference was gone" when her older sister developed schizophrenia. Twenty years later, her sister is happily married, holding a good computer job, and living "an incredibly normal life": "Our relationship is great — we have the same sister feelings we had before her illness."

OFFSPRING

Because of their young age and the significance of the parent-child bond, offspring may be the most vulnerable family members. After all, parents reside at the center of our earliest relationship, are essential for our survival, strongly influence our feelings about ourselves, act as role models and agents of socialization, and serve as a link to our ancestral history. In the words of one woman whose mother had mental illness, "I have been burned to my very core."

Clearly, the impact of parental mental illness is immense for their children. Important offspring themes include grief and loss, offspring survivor's guilt, parentification, caregiving, and the personal legacy. The potential losses of offspring are enormous. They may mourn for their own losses — of love, comfort, guidance, companionship, validation, and protection — and for the losses experienced by their beloved parent. Offspring may also mourn for their well parent: "My dad also abandoned us, in the emotional sense, becoming so confused and devastated that he was oblivious to our feelings and unable to help us deal with them." Ultimately, they may mourn for the very loss of their childhood: "I can honestly say I have no idea what it is like to be a child."

Parentification is perhaps the most salient dimension of the offspring experience. Professionals[17] and offspring alike note the risk that they will assume a parental role as they are growing up: "I had to be the little mother, since I was the oldest girl." Transfused as it is by the parent-child bond, offspring survivor's guilt rings with a singular resonance. "She was the mother who had given me life," one daughter wrote. "Somehow, I thought to myself, I had to bring her happiness."[18] Often, they become "perfect" children — the "invulnerable children"[19] so prevalent in the professional literature: "As a child I tried desperately never to have a problem because our family had so many. So I became perfectionistic and hid my fears, concerns, and needs from everyone."

Although caregiving is a central theme for all family members, only offspring are likely to assume caregiving roles from their earliest years and to remain in those roles for a lifetime. One adult offspring recalled becoming the sole caregiver for a mother with schizophrenia at age 8 after her father's death. By the time she was 12, she had hospitalized her mother for the first time. For the next 6 years she battled the hospitals, the courts, and the landlords, until her mother's death in a state hospital. "My whole childhood was spent taking care of others," she has written. Another woman assumed a caregiving role during adolescence:

> When I was 18, I became my mother's caretaker. My mother lived with me until she died. I married, had children, and took care of Mother throughout my whole life. That placed our family under severe emotional stress. Every ordinarily stressful life experience precipitated a crisis in which Mother's hallucinations or delusions were exacerbated.

As with siblings, offspring experience a personal legacy that pervades all the crawl spaces of their lives. As young family members, they may become enveloped in their parent's psychotic system, have difficulty establishing a secure sense of self, and lose touch with their own needs and feelings: "I lost the ability to feel for so many years. It was the only way I could protect myself and survive." Their academic lives and peer relationships may also suffer: "I had trouble concentrating in school, was afraid Dad would appear at the school grounds when he was sick."

As adults, offspring may have difficulty establishing independent lives: "I had completely lost the thread of my own life." Because our earliest relationships serve as templates for those in the future, their adult relationships may be troubled: "I still have a tendency to hold back in relationships for fear that I will be abandoned. Somehow I still feel like that little girl who had to take care of everything herself." One adult offspring described himself as "a person who fears close relationships but longs for them daily"; another wrote, "I avoid intimacy but crave it desperately. I want more friends but fear to trust." At the same time, offspring frequently develop qualities that endear them to others. Their tolerance, empathy, and compassion are likely to make them valued and sympathetic friends.

When they marry, often with a fervent desire to create a new and more perfect family, offspring often have few relevant role models and skills: "My only role model was a schizophrenic mother." Contemplating parenthood, they are likely to worry about the risk of mental illness in the next generation: "I was afraid to have children because I had a fear that they might be like my dad." Throughout their lives, offspring worry about their own mental health, vigilant for signs that they too may develop serious mental illness.

As with all family members, however, parents and offspring are a diverse group. Not all parents with mental illness are ineffective parents, nor do all of their offspring suffer such adverse consequences. Even when paying a very high price for a parent with mental illness, offspring may derive much satisfaction from this primal relationship: "I feel that being a concerned family member has helped me become a better person in many ways. I learned to become self-sufficient at an early age. I am gratified that I helped my mother."

IMPLICATIONS FOR INTERVENTION

Parents, spouses, siblings, and offspring share the oppressive family burden and the essential family needs. Accordingly, these family members can all benefit from the interventions described earlier in the book, including family consultation, support groups, education, psychoeducation, and psychotherapy. In addition, each role carries implications for professional practice.

Adult Family Members. The family interventions described earlier in the book were primarily designed to address the needs of parents, the most frequent participants in family-focused programs. Thus, these interventions are already adapted to address parental needs and concerns. Such is not the case for spouses.

Services for spouses are a cost-effective means of strengthening families and meeting the needs of their individual members. Yet specialized services for spouses are rarely available, and parent-oriented services often fail to address their concerns. In the words of one wife, "If spouses go to parent-oriented groups, rest assured that they WILL NOT return, as there is nothing for them!" As Edie Mannion[20] has pointed out, parent-oriented programs might focus on parental concern about continuity of caregiving for their son or daughter following their own death or decline. In contrast, spouses might need immediate assistance in compensating for their partner's impaired functioning, protecting themselves and their children during a partner's manic episodes, or preventing personal financial ruin due to the legal liabilities of marriage.

What *is* likely to be helpful is family consultation, which can assist spouses to identify and prioritize their marital, parental, and personal needs, and to deal with illness-related concerns. Some spouse support groups are available through NAMI and the National Depressive and Manic Depressive Association. In addition, Mannion[21] has developed a Spouse Coping Skills Workshop, as well as a facilitator's manual, reporting that spousal participation results in increased knowledge of mental illness and coping strategies, and in decreased personal distress and negative attitudes toward the partner.

Spouses also may find individual and couple therapy beneficial. One woman told me that the most important aspect of her own recovery was personal therapy that helped her find herself in a life that can be "crazy-making" for spouses. Another echoed, "The therapist can help well spouses find themselves again." Clinicians can also help spouses make difficult decisions about their marriage. Some spouses may need assistance to remain in the marriage; others may need help in leaving.

Similarly, couple therapy can be very beneficial. Affirming its benefits, one spouse observed, "As a result, we aren't just married; we are building a good working, loving relationship."[22] Mannion[23] cautions that effective couple therapy requires that (a) the partner's illness be stabilized; (b) the partner acknowledge the illness; (c) both members of the couple be committed to trying couple therapy; and (d) the therapist have special expertise in mental illness. When these conditions are met, Mannion has found that couple therapy can help the couple "get reacquainted" after the trauma of an acute episode of mental illness, deal with symptom-related problems, learn to communicate about the illness, establish appropriate family roles and relationships, and reestablish trust so they can unite against the illness.

Young Family Members. Young siblings and offspring have compelling needs from the moment that mental illness appears in their families. Accordingly, practitioners should reach out to young family members as early as possible to acknowledge their anguish, to address their needs, and to assist them in coping with this family catastrophe. Likewise, services should be appropriate for their developmental level and responsive to their changing needs throughout their lives.

As young family members, they need three kinds of services: for their relative with mental illness, for their family as a unit, and for themselves. As patients with serious mental illness recover, the entire family benefits. Likewise, siblings and offspring need services that can support and strengthen their family, which is their most important resource as they are growing up. Helpful family services might include a home-based program, parenting classes for parents with mental illness, supported housing for families, and respite care during periods of crisis.

At every developmental phase, siblings and offspring have needs for age-appropriate information, coping skills, and support. For example, they may need:

- reassurance that their needs matter;
- simple and direct explanations of mental illness;
- encouragement to ask questions and express their feelings;
- assurance that they are not to blame;
- practical suggestions for dealing with the illness;
- assistance in developing a satisfactory relationship with their relative;
- support for their school work and peer relationships;
- encouragement to participate in activities outside the home; and
- help in developing constructive long-term plans.

A range of services may meet these needs, including programs designed to strengthen family relationships during crises or periods of hospitalization, provider-based educational programs and support groups for young family members, school-based educational programs or groups for children and adolescents, and individual sessions with school psychologists or mental health professionals. Although programs for young family members are relatively rare, some excellent programs have been developed.[24]

In reality, however, few siblings and offspring of any age have access to specialized programs. As one sibling complained, "You don't get professional help and support. You're not given any guidance. You are left floundering." Similar frustration is expressed by offspring: "The mental health field provided me with no resources for coping. The professionals focused on my father's treatment as if he were an island, while my mother, my brothers, and myself suffered from invisibility."[25]

When they *do* receive patient-oriented services, siblings and offspring often find these services unhelpful at best and harmful at worst. In her interviews with family members, Mona Wasow[26] heard from siblings who had been subject to "family bashing" that took place in family therapy, locked up in the hospital with the patient for therapy, videotaped in family therapy by a "show-off" therapist, and refused information under the guise of confidentiality. My own contacts have elicited similar complaints:

> I was 16 when my 14-year-old brother had his first psychotic episode. His illness was the most devastating episode of my entire life. I was ashamed, I was afraid, I was confused. I was involved in family therapy sessions that put the blame on the family. It was awful.

An adult offspring expressed comparable resentment: "We had one family therapy session behind a one-way mirror with people gawking at us. I just hated it."[27]

In contrast to these negative perceptions, when siblings and offspring receive services for themselves, such as psychotherapy, their perceptions are generally very positive. As already mentioned, a majority of adult siblings and offspring who participated in our survey[28] had sought personal therapy. These family members almost always found it very helpful: "It wasn't until I sought therapy for anxiety upon my divorce that I began to understand some of the dynamics of my family and myself. Therapy opened doors to my self and answered many puzzling questions."

In spite of the potential for professional services to meet the needs of these vulnerable family members, far too many share the following view: "I don't think anything has helped." In the words of one woman who grew up with parental mental illness, "There are many children out there who are suffering the way that my sisters and brother and I suffered. There has to be a way to reach them."

COPING WITH CHALLENGES

When I offer training to front-line providers, such as case managers or family advocates, I invariably hear about the challenges that arise in professional practice with families. These might include patient challenges, such as resistance to family involvement; family challenges, such as the patient's treatment nonadherence or substance abuse; or professional challenges, such as family hostility or disengagement. These challenges, along with suggestions for their resolution, are the focus of the present section.[1]

PATIENT CHALLENGES

Although most patients do not object to professional contacts with their families, some do express strong opposition. This opposition has many sources, including paranoid symptoms directed toward family members, maltreatment on the part of the family, or the healthy desire of patients for autonomy. Some problems, such as persistent paranoia, are best managed by the patient's treatment team, which may profit from family input.

Other problems, such as a family environment that poses risks for the patient — and perhaps for other family members — may require practitioners to take protective action. In one situation, each time a patient returned from a home visit with his substance-abusing and sometimes violent family, he suffered symptom exacerbation. With the patient's agreement and the family's concurrence, the practitioner began planning for his eventual release to a community residence, where weekend visits proceeded without incident.

Still other problems, such as the patient's desire for autonomy, may be best approached by working jointly with the patient and family. Because the onset of serious mental illness often occurs in late adolescence or early adulthood, the illness typically disrupts the normal process of separation and autonomy. As patients begin to recover, they are likely to resume their developmental journey, however off-time. In recent years, the "awakenings" experienced by patients in response to the newer medications illustrate this pattern, sometimes many years after the onset of the illness.

Such awakenings may pose problems for both patients and families. As noted earlier, there are real risks that accompany recovery. Patients may feel "stuck" in an earlier phase of development that leaves them out-of-sync with their age cohort. Or they may be plunged into a debilitating depression when their new-found lucidity heightens their awareness of the immense toll exacted by the illness. The patient's treatment team may be able to offer assistance in dealing with such recovery-related issues.

At the same time, providers may be able to help families understand their relative's recovery process and assume a less crisis-oriented and protective role. There may have been genuine risks in the past that have left families with a compelling need to ensure the patient's safety. Although understandable, such overprotectiveness on the part of families may conflict with the needs of recovering patients to manage their illness and their lives, to take risks and learn from their mistakes, to move outside the family circle, and to revive earlier vocational plans. Assured that there are now other sources of patient support, most families can learn to relinquish earlier attitudes and behaviors that are no longer appropriate.

On the other hand, some patients — often late adolescents or young adults — may adamantly refuse any family involvement, perhaps threatening to terminate treatment if their wishes are not honored. In such cases, parents who receive an explanation and a referral to other resources are likely to respect a professional recommendation that their involvement in the patient's treatment is clinically unwise, at least for the present. Over time, some accommodation can usually be reached. In other cases, alternative living arrangements may be appropriate.

FAMILY CHALLENGES

Families of patients with serious mental illness are likely to face a daunting array of challenges. Over the years, they may need to cope with:

- positive and negative symptoms;
- manic and depressive episodes;
- recurrent crises;
- treatment nonadherence;
- potentially self-destructive or violent behavior;
- substance abuse;
- setting limits; and
- long-term planning.

I will briefly discuss each of these family challenges. Some excellent resources[2] are available to assist families, including *Bipolar Disorder: A Guide for Patients and Families* by Francis Mondimore; *Coping With Schizophrenia: A Guide for Families* by Kim Mueser and Susan Gingerich, and *Surviving Schizophrenia: A Manual for Families, Consumers and Providers* by E. Fuller Torrey.

Schizophrenia is often associated with a range of positive symptoms, such as hallucinations and delusions, and of negative symptoms, such as apathy and amotivation. Practitioners can educate families about these symptoms and encourage them to speak with their relative about his or her experience of mental illness, to respond nonjudgmentally without reinforcing the symptoms, and to consult with the patient's treatment team about the best way to respond. For example, when the patient complains of hearing voices, a family member might say,"I'd be worried too if I heard those voices. Is there anything I can do to help?" In the case of negative symptoms, families might encourage the patient to become involved in activities outside the family, such as a consumer support group or drop-in center.

Families that are dealing with manic or depressive episodes need to learn about the symptoms of mood disorders, to distinguish between symptoms and normal moods, and to identify the warning signs of an impending episode. Professionals can also help families to understand medication issues, such as the reluctance of some patients to relinquish the "highs" of mania; to establish controls (e.g., with spending sprees); to avoid escalations; and to avoid taking illness-related behavior personally. When coping with severe depression, it is helpful for families to offer concrete help, such as assistance with shopping or meal preparation.

Families also need to identify the signs of impending crisis, such as sudden changes in behavior or biological rhythms, or increases in anxiety or hostility. They need to have contingency plans available, including emergency contacts and phone numbers, and to discuss these plans with the patient. Depending on their circumstances, these plans may include contacts in the legal or criminal justice systems. Practitioners can help families learn to remain calm during a crisis, to defuse the crisis when possible, to approach the crisis in a firm and loving manner, and to separate the person from the symptoms. Medication adherence is also important.

Especially at the onset of the patient's illness, families often complain about treatment nonadherence, such as failure to take medication or follow through with scheduled appointments. Clinicians can help families understand possible reasons for nonadherence, including patient denial of the illness, the presence of symptoms that interfere with rational thinking, intolerable side effects of medication, and patient perception that treatment has a negative impact on quality of life. Families can benefit from knowledge of current treatments, including new medications. If forgetfulness is a problem, injectables may offer a solution. Patients are most likely to take prescribed medication when they play a role in choosing the most appropriate medication and determining the lowest effective dose.

In the case of potentially self-destructive or violent behavior, families need to learn the warning signs, such as expressions of hopelessness or hostility, verbal threats, changes in biological rhythms, an increase of symptoms, or the presence of command hallucinations that encourage suicidal or violent behavior. A history of such behavior increases the current risk, as does the presence of a plan. Professionals can help families learn to respond to their relative in a calm and supportive manner, to defuse crises, to offer concrete assistance to the patient, and to obtain emergency assistance. Family members should leave the scene immediately if they feel in danger.

Over the course of their lives, half of patients with serious mental illness will have a co-occurring substance abuse problem.[3] The incidence of such comorbidity is approximately 25% at any given time. Families need to learn about this dual diagnosis and about the adverse consequences of substance use on the course of mental illness. They also need to understand possible reasons for substance use, including patient efforts to reduce symptoms or medication side effects through self-medication, to improve their social life and reduce feelings of isolation, or to anesthetize the anguish and hopelessness so often experienced in mental illness. In severe cases, substances may ward off withdrawal symptoms. Practitioners can assist families to maintain communication with the patient, to encourage the patient to obtain appropriate treatment, to understand the high risk of relapse, and to take action themselves, such as joining Al-Anon or setting firm limits regarding substance use in the home.

Limit setting is important for all families. No one should have to live in a disturbing or dangerous environment. Professionals can assist families to decide which behaviors are unacceptable and should not be tolerated, such as behavior that is abusive, self-destructive, harmful to others, damaging to property, or severely disruptive. The next step is to set clear limits for the patient and to impose consequences when those limits are exceeded. Families also need to decide which behaviors can be ignored, such as those that are merely annoying or embarrassing. Family members may likewise need to set personal limits, maintaining a comfortable level of involvement in the patient's life as well as a satisfying life of their own.

Especially among aging parents who serve as primary caregivers for the patient, long-term planning may be a central concern. In fact, such planning is often important in dealing with serious mental illness, which is by definition severe and persistent. Clinicians can encourage families to have an open and continuing dialogue about planning that involves the patient to the extent possible. Patients with serious mental illness are generally eligible for a range of benefits, including Social Security Disability Insurance (SSDI), Supplementary Security Income (SSI), and public assistance (welfare), as well as associated health care and other benefits. Information from local agencies can help families ensure that long-term plans do not jeopardize eligibility for these benefits.

Families may also profit from information about community resources, such as residential options, and from consultation with a lawyer who is knowledgeable about estate planning for people with disabilities. To avoid jeopardizing the patient's eligibility for benefits, some families may decide to establish a trust fund and appoint a trustee to administer the trust. The trustee, either an individual or financial institution, distributes funds based on the specific provisions of the trust.

A given family may need to become familiar with procedures for establishing health care proxy (concerned with treatment decisions) and durable power of attorney (concerned with legal and financial matters); and for appointment of a guardian (with authority over personal and financial decisions) or conservator (with authority over property and money issues). Another useful resource is NAMI, which can provide information about long-term planning.

PROFESSIONAL CHALLENGES

When working with these families, practitioners sometimes face challenges of their own. For instance, they may need to deal with family denial, anger, conflict, overinvolvement, demoralization, and disengagement. Such family patterns may be either a manifestation of the family's characteristic mode of functioning or an exaggerated response to the illness. Especially at its onset, many family members respond to mental illness with disbelief, intense negative emotions, and family strife; they often oscillate between overinvolvement and disengagement; and they are periodically subject to feelings of demoralization.

Although understandable, these family patterns can pose significant problems when they persist, when they seriously undermine family functioning, and when they interfere with patient recovery. The family interventions already discussed may assist some of these troubled families to modify their attitudes and behaviors in constructive ways, although progress is frequently slow and uneven. I will briefly discuss each of these family patterns and offer some suggestions.

Denial and disbelief are common responses during the initial phase of family adaptation. As Kayla Bernheim and Anthony Lehman[4] have counseled, family members should not be pushed into giving up their denial prematurely (or entirely), but can be helped to adapt in spite of their need to protect themselves from the harsh reality of serious mental illness. As they learn more about the illness, some family members may develop more hopeful attitudes. Others may never fully accept the mental illness or may require an extended period of time before relinquishing their early denial. Thus, a given family may include members with varying degrees of denial and acceptance. Recognizing the protective function of their adaptation, professionals can allow family members to set their own pace and assist them in finding an appropriate balance between denying and overemphasizing the illness.

Anger is often present in these families and may derive from many sources, such as a phase in the family grieving process. Likewise, family members may direct their anger at many targets: at God or fate for the injustice visited on the family, at the patient for symptomatic behavior or for simply failing to get better, at other family members under conditions of severe stress, at themselves for actual mistakes or human fallibility, or at professionals for genuine deficiencies or a shortage of miracles. Therapists can offer families an opportunity to express anger and to gain insight into its roots. At the same time, families can be encouraged to channel their anger in more constructive directions, such as advocacy.

As noted earlier, mental illness creates fertile ground for conflict, especially at the onset of the illness. Family members may disagree about the diagnosis, the treatment plan, the roles and responsibilities of particular family members, the best ways of managing the illness, and their relationships with professionals. Given the high level of stress associated with the illness, any preexisting conflicts are likely to be exacerbated under these circumstances, siphoning energy that is needed for effective family functioning, undermining family relationships, and interfering with the patient's recovery. Clinicians can encourage family members to understand each other's views and to resolve their differences in a mutually tolerant and respectful manner. Family sessions might enhance the family's communication and problem-solving skills.

Overinvolvement is an understandable response to mental illness, especially among parents who serve as primary caregivers, often with little professional support and guidance. Over the course of the illness, family members may experience repeated crises, frightening psychotic episodes, difficulty accessing appropriate treatment, and possibly homelessness, suicide attempts, violence, or incarceration. Mindful of these potential hazards, they may circle the wagons in an effort to preserve their relative's safety and perhaps his or her life. At the same time, overprotectiveness may hinder the patient's recovery as well as the autonomy of other family members. Professionals can educate families about the illness and community resources, assisting them to find a meaningful and appropriate role in their relative's treatment and recovery. That role will vary across families, whose adaptation may range from a high level of interdependence to a more "loving distance"[5] marked by greater autonomy.

The experience of demoralization is a common one, as families struggle with intense feelings of grief and loss, symptomatic behavior, caregiving responsibilities, limitations of the service delivery system, and social stigma. Faced with this often-unrelenting burden, it is no wonder that most families occasionally appear disheartened and debilitated. For some families, however, demoralization calcifies into a state of paralysis that prevents them from supporting their relative's recovery and from moving on with their own lives. Providers can provide information about effective treatment and the prospects for a positive outcome, encouraging families to maintain a hopeful attitude.

Disengagement is also an understandable family response, especially after many years of living with the mental illness and its aftermath. Witnessing — and perhaps feeling victimized by — their relative's bizarre, inappropriate, or destructive behavior, families may assume the behavior is both willful and hostile. Feeling exhausted and helpless, they may decide their very survival depends on terminating their relationship with the patient, especially if professional support is unavailable. Yet caring families are likely to experience substantial guilt if they terminate their relationship, leaving a void in the family that lasts for a lifetime. With the assistance of professionals, these families may be able to view troublesome symptoms in a less personal way and to develop a plan that allows them to honor their commitment to their relative without sacrificing lives of their own. An individualized family service plan may offer considerable help.

SUGGESTIONS FOR PRACTITIONERS

When faced with these and other challenges, clinicians need to recognize that most families are struggling to do their best under daunting circumstances. Using a flexible and individualized approach, clinicians can strive to understand each family's history and current situation, to accept each family on its own terms, and to respect their unique adaptations and responses. For a given family, it might be best to establish a workable alliance with selected members who can guide others in the family, to initiate a structured process of successive approximation that assists families in reaching appropriate goals in a step-by-step fashion, or to help the family develop a nontraditional network of close friends, neighbors, and church members.

The more defensive, hostile, or disengaged the family, the more important it is for professionals to serve as a cornerstone of their support network. As Susan McDaniel and her colleagues[6] have observed, families have a need for the communion found in emotional bonds, which can be all but sundered by illness. Defining communion as a restoration of human connections, they encourage professionals to counteract the collective isolation imposed by the illness and assist families in recapturing their affection, humor, common interests, and mutual respect:

> Family members may be stuck together in a tight clump of single-minded preoccupation with the illness and its costs, while at the same time feeling deeply isolated from one another. Their love and concern for one another can become fused with guilt, anguish, resentment and depression that completely distort the quality of family life.

Providers need to emphasize the potential of services to support and empower families. Bernheim and Lehman[7] have pointed out that the attitude "What can we do *for you*?" works much better than "What are *you going to do* for the patient?" As their needs are met, troubled families are likely to be less defensive, angry, and demoralized. In turn, the decrease in family defensiveness and rigidity increases their potential for learning and change. Permitting families to set their own pace and agenda, professionals can encourage them to gradually alter their attitudes, expectations, and behaviors.

Not all families are willing or able to modify their maladaptive patterns or to play a constructive role in their relative's life. Where family hostility and conflict remain entrenched, for example, the patient may need alternative living arrangements and sources of social support. As Bernheim and Lehman[8] have written, "Every family deserves a chance, and every clinician has the right and responsibility to say 'enough is enough.'" Working in this challenging area, clinicians need to protect themselves by recognizing their own limitations, practicing good self-care, making necessary referrals, consulting with knowledgeable colleagues, and cultivating their personal support network.

In summary, practitioners can help these families modify their inappropriate response to their relative's illness by:

- fostering family engagement;
- reframing these patterns from the family's perspective;
- focusing on the concerns of families themselves;
- addressing their needs for information, skills, and support;
- serving as a cornerstone of their support system;
- respecting their particular adaptation and pace;
- assisting them to channel their negative emotions in constructive ways;
- helping them to separate their relative from the illness;
- encouraging them to maintain satisfying lives of their own; and
- reinforcing a sense of hopefulness.

PROFESSIONAL ISSUES

This final section is concerned with the ethical and legal context of professional practice. Following a brief overview of general considerations, I will address several topics of particular importance in practice with families of patients who have serious mental illness. These include competence, confidentiality, relationships, informed consent, and diagnosis and reimbursement in family practice. The section ends with some suggestions for practitioners.

ETHICAL AND LEGAL CONSIDERATIONS

In a recent article, Nancy Hansen and Susan Goldberg[1] specified the ethical and legal issues that merit consideration in professional practice: (a) moral principles and personal values; (b) clinical and cultural factors; (c) the professional code of ethics; (d) agency or employer policies; (e) federal, state, and local statues; (f) rules and regulations; and (g) case law. Although each mental health discipline has its own professional code of ethics, this general structure is applicable across disciplines. In a given case, some of these considerations may be more important than others.

The first consideration is moral principles and personal values. Moral principles are the enduring beliefs and modes of conduct that protect the interests and welfare of all involved. Hansen and Goldberg list five principles:

- Beneficence: promoting the welfare of others (the core duty)
- Fidelity: fulfilling implicit or explicit promises (e.g., confidentiality)
- Autonomy: providing meaningful informed consent
- Justice: ensuring fair distribution of benefits (e.g., impoverished clients)
- Nonmalfeasance: not harming others (the overarching concern)

Personal values are also important, including religious and political values. So, too, are the values included in some professional ethical codes. For example, the code of the American Psychological Association (APA)[2] mentions competence, integrity, responsibility, concern for other's welfare, and social responsibility.

The second consideration is clinical factors, including clinical perception and judgment (e.g., competence and the need for consultation), and cultural factors, such as cultural identification and cultural mores.

Third, practitioners need to be familiar with their professional code of ethics. The APA code includes 104 enforceable ethical standards. As Hansen and Goldberg note, professional codes may contain potentially contradictory mandates and often fail to address or anticipate current or emerging issues.

Fourth, practitioners need to be aware of agency or employer policies. These might include policies of military or correctional facilities or of managed care companies, along with procedures concerning such matters as confidential information, record keeping, and client access to files. Hansen and Goldberg observe that major tensions may arise when the payer of services is not the patient. When conflicts do arise, the APA code indicates that psychologists must attempt resolution; they need not resign if they are unsuccessful.

The fifth consideration is federal, state, and local statutes, which may mandate or prohibit behavior. For instance, state statutes may cover confidentiality, privilege, involuntary commitment, age of consent, access to records, rights of nonclients, duty to protect, duty to report abuse, practices of managed care organizations, or prohibitions on sexual relations. County ordinances may address other issues, such as limiting the extent of professional use of a home residence.

Sixth, professionals need to be aware of relevant rules and regulations. Federal, state, or local statues might provide implementation rules or regulations that elaborate, explain, and sometimes modify the law. An example is the Department of Health and Human Services Regulations that pertain to confidentiality in federally funded substance abuse programs. There are also codes of conduct that implement state licensing laws.

The seventh consideration is case law, including federal and state court rulings found in published reports of decisions, as well as torts (negligent or intentional actions that cause harm) governed by common law. Case law also covers malpractice, which pertains when a professional treats a patient negligently, or fails to treat a patient according to accepted standards of care. Hansen and Goldberg note that the client will prevail in malpractice cases if (a) the jury is persuaded that the clinician had a duty to the client, (b) the duty is breached, and (c) the actions (or inactions) were the "proximate cause" of harm or injury to client. Grounds for malpractice may include failure to obtain informed consent, improper diagnosis, negligent treatment, failure to prevent harm, sexual relations with the client, or inappropriate referral, supervision, or consultation.

All in all, a daunting compendium of legal and ethical considerations! From the perspective of risk management, several strategies can assist professionals to avoid ethical and legal problems. As Richard

Magee and I note in the introduction to our book *Ethical and Legal Issues in Professional Practice With Families*,[3] practitioners should be knowledgeable about their professional code of ethics and about applicable federal and state law; consult with colleagues as appropriate; establish positive and collaborative relationships with clients and their families; communicate effectively about ethical matters to relevant parties; anticipate problems and develop strategies for their resolution; document treatment carefully; and remain abreast of current theory and research to ensure that their treatment is appropriate and effective.

In addition to continuing education and professional publications concerned with ethical and legal issues, clinicians may have other resources available, such as the legal consultation plan available to members through the Pennsylvania Psychological Association. It is also important to be familiar with the process of ethical decision making, because ethical dilemmas frequently arise in professional practice. Decision-making models[4] typically include the following steps: (a) Describe pertinent variables in the situation; (b) define the potential legal and ethical issues involved; (c) consult relevant guidelines; (d) evaluate the rights, responsibilities, and welfare of all affected parties; (e) generate alternative solutions; (f) numerate anticipated consequences of each, including its likelihood of occurrence; (g) make a decision; and (h) evaluate the outcome.

Turning now to the ethical and legal considerations of particular importance in the area of serious mental illness, I will begin with the following vignette:

> Peter Hogan is a 19-year-old student who has just been admitted to the psychiatric unit of the medical facility associated with his university. Although this is Peter's first contact with the mental health system, for several months he has been hearing voices and claiming that unnamed people are plotting against him. At first, his family and friends ascribed his increasingly erratic behavior and lack of focus to academic pressures. But after Peter began conversing with himself in public, the resident assistant in his dorm brought him to the medical center emergency room. In light of Peter's psychotic symptoms, the physician on duty transferred him to the psychiatric unit. Staff psychologist Joan Montoya has been assigned to meet with

Peter's concerned parents. What professional issues merit consideration in this case?

In answering this question, I will incorporate material from the APA ethics code, although codes of other disciplines include similar material.

PROFESSIONAL COMPETENCIES[5]

All mental health professionals are mandated by their ethical codes to maintain minimal standards of competence, to recognize the boundaries of their competence, and to provide only those services for which they are qualified. In working with the Hogans and other similar families, practitioners need certain knowledge, skills, and attitudes. In addition to general clinical competence, professionals also need specialized knowledge, including current understanding of serious mental illness, family experiences and needs, competence-based and collaborative approaches, effective family interventions, and community resources. Specialized skills are also essential, including skills that can enhance stress management, communication, problem solving, consensus building, illness management, and relapse prevention. Facilitative attitudes include tolerance, respect, and compassion.

Returning to the Hogan family, all of these competencies are important. In the initial session, Dr. Montoya will need to provide information about Peter's symptoms, diagnosis, treatment plan, and prognosis, as well as available services and resources. She also should be aware of the potential impact of Peter's illness on his family, including any siblings. Working in partnership with the family, Dr. Montoya must be able to promote family engagement, to conduct a family assessment, and to develop and implement a family service plan. She also needs to deal with several professional issues, including confidentiality, relationships, and informed consent.

CONFIDENTIALITY[6]

Professionals often view confidentiality as a rigid barrier to working with families. Yet such a stance is rarely in the best interest of patients, family members, or providers. Thus, it is essential for clinicians to understand potential conflicts regarding confidentiality and the ways in which these conflicts can be resolved. Ethical codes of mental health professionals protect the right of patients to a confidential therapeutic relationship. At the same time, families also have rights, particularly if they are serving as primary caregivers.

Several strategies can assist practitioners to resolve the potential conflict between the patient's right to confidentiality and the needs of families. Initially, it is important to distinguish between confidential and nonconfidential information. Much information regarding serious mental illness is available to the general public and can be shared with families, including information about diagnostic categories, etiology, symptoms, treatment, medication, and prognosis. Such nonconfidential information is essential for family members, who can benefit from written materials and educational programs.

When confidentiality does pertain, professionals can use a release of information form specifically designed for families (see below). If the release form is presented at the right time (when the patient is able to provide informed consent) and in the right manner (as something to enhance treatment), most patients are willing to authorize the release of relevant information to their families. In the Pittsburgh area, for example, where there are standard confidentiality procedures in the public mental health system, 90% of patients choose to sign the release form.

RELEASE OF INFORMATION FORM

CONSENT TO RELEASE
CONFIDENTIAL INFORMATION TO FAMILY MEMBERS

NAME: _____

DOB: _____ SS#: _____

I hereby request and authorize (SPECIFY PROVIDER) _____
_____ to release information regarding me to the individual(s) listed below. I understand that the purpose of this release is to improve communication between the above-named agency and the individual(s) listed below and to assist in my treatment. Treatment began at this agency on (SPECIFY DATE)_____.

****

I hereby request and authorize you to release the information indicated below to the following individual(s) (SPECIFY NAME/RELATIONSHIP):

_____

_____

You have my permission to release the following information (check all that apply):

❐ Name of Therapist   ❐ Psychological Evaluation
❐ Name of Case Manager   ❐ Scheduled Appointments
❐ Treatment Programs(s)   ❐ Medication
❐ Treatment Plan   ❐ Admission to/Discharge from Any Facility
❐ Treatment Summary   ❐ Discharge Plans
❐ Progress Notes
❐ Other (SPECIFY): _____

_____

****

I understand that this gives my consent for the release of information to the individual(s) listed above. I also understand that this allows the above-mentioned individual(s) to provide information to my therapist or case manager. I may revoke this release at any time except to the extent that the person who is to make the disclosure has already acted upon it. Except as noted above, this release will expire on (SPECIFY DATE) _____ or under the following circumstances: _____
_____.

_____   _____
Witness #1   Date

_____   _____
Patient   Date

_____   _____
Witness #2   Date

_____   _____
Patient   Date

(Second witness needed if patient is unable to give verbal consent.)

Practitioners can also serve as mediators, negotiating the boundaries of confidentiality to meet the needs of particular patients and families. Therapists can discuss with patients the importance of keeping their families informed and can work with both parties in deciding what — and how — specific information will be shared. In group practice or institutional settings, separate staff members can serve as family advocates who provide relevant information to families and consult with the treatment team to enhance treatment planning and coordination. With the consent of the patient, families may become actively involved in treatment, perhaps as members of the treatment team. As active participants, family members can offer suggestions, play a meaningful role in decisions that affect them, and share observations about the risk of imminent harm and other serious matters.

Even when confidentiality pertains, clinicians are not prohibited from listening to family members, although it may be clinically unwise in certain cases. Even when practitioners feel it is best not to have contact with families (perhaps to protect a fragile therapeutic relationship), they should ensure that families have an avenue to express their concerns and observations. One mother I know tried unsuccessfully to communicate her concern about her daughter's potential for a suicide attempt, which might have been avoided with better communication.

Several additional considerations deserve attention. Patients can always reveal information to their families and can also assign that role to their therapists by signing a release form. Thus, as early as possible professionals should encourage patients to make an informed choice about the information that will be shared with family members and the ways in which information will be shared. Furthermore, consent requires competence, so the decision should be deferred if the patient is experiencing severe psychotic symptoms. Other ethical principles may conflict with (and take precedence over) confidentiality, including the risk of imminent harm to the patient or to others. Faced with such risks, professionals may be ethically and legally required to contact family members.

Because Peter Hogan is an adult, it is best if Dr. Montoya discusses confidentiality with him before meeting with his family. Following the process just described, she explains the principle of confidentiality to Peter, emphasizes the value of involving his parents in his treatment, and assists him in completing a release form that specifies what information will be shared with his parents (e.g., the diagnosis and treatment plan, but not therapy sessions), and how that information will be shared (e.g., verbally). Then, at her meeting with Peter's parents, Dr. Montoya can inform them about confidentiality before conducting the initial consultative session. Should a conflict arise between Peter and his parents, such as their interest in knowing something he prefers not to reveal, the practitioner can work with both parties in resolving the conflict. If Peter returns home after his hospitalization but continues in outpatient treatment, confidentiality should be revisited to accommodate the altered circumstances.

RELATIONSHIPS

Practitioners who work with these families need to clarify at the outset which family members are clients, the nature of the relationship with each family member, and policies regarding communication with members who are not clients. For example, when therapists are offering services to patients with mental illness, they may have collateral contacts with families that focus on history taking, crisis intervention, and telephone contact. Providers may also work with families as clients themselves who receive consultative, educational, skills-oriented, or psychotherapeutic services. As already discussed, professional roles vary significantly across these family interventions. Before working with families, clinicians need to clarify their own role, as well as the role of the family in the patient's treatment plan.

When working with Mr. and Mrs. Hogan, Dr. Montoya should establish the nature of their relationship with Peter's treatment team. She should also clarify the differences in both professional and client roles across various family services.

INFORMED CONSENT

Mental health professionals are required to obtain appropriate informed consent to therapy or related procedures, using language that is reasonably understandable to participants. When working with families, clinicians can assist them in making an informed decision about their use of services by discussing the available services, their potential risks and benefits, the risks of forgoing services, and possible alternatives. Research support for various services might also be shared with families. For example, given the strong evidence that a stressful family environment can increase the risk of patient relapse, some families might be encouraged to participate in a psychoeducational program designed to help them reduce their level of ambient stress.

In the case of Peter Hogan, following her family assessment, let us assume that Dr. Montoya is concerned about the tendency of his parents to respond to Peter in a critical, hostile, and intrusive manner. She is aware that these behaviors may increase the risk of relapse for Peter, and that participation in a family psychoeducation program may help the Hogans provide a more supportive home environment. During several consultative sessions, Dr. Montoya educates Peter's parents about his mental illness and the risks associated with a high-stress environment. She describes the available family interventions, as well as their potential risks and benefits. Dr. Montoya recommends that the Hogans participate in a multifamily psychoeducational program and shares her rationale with the parents. Although willing to follow her recommendation, the parents request periodic consultative sessions that can address their particular concerns. They also plan to participate in a support group offered by the local NAMI affiliate.

DIAGNOSIS AND REIMBURSEMENT

Diagnosis and reimbursement often pose problems for providers who offer services to couples and families. Professional and managed care organizations generally assume an individual model of practice that generalizes only partly to multiperson therapies. In addition, although professional practice with couples and families often focuses on distressed relationships, present diagnostic systems do not include relational disorders, a term used to describe problems in relationships.

As Florence Kaslow[7] has discussed, family practitioners consequently face the dilemma of providing a diagnosis that accurately reflects relational problems without neglecting individual clients and without committing insurance fraud. Consider the case of a husband and wife whose individual problems do not meet the criteria for a *Diagnostic and Statistical Manual of Mental Disorders (DSM-IV)*[8] diagnosis, but who have sought therapy to deal with significant marital conflict. The widespread practice of giving individual diagnoses in such cases misrepresents the focus and method of treatment and raises both ethical and legal concerns.

In Kaslow's[9] edited book *Handbook of Relational Diagnosis and Dysfunctional Family Patterns*, Terence Patterson and Don-David

Lusterman[10] offer an incisive analysis of the "relational reimbursement dilemma," noting that practitioners of couple, family, and parent-child therapy frequently have a need to provide formal diagnosis for reimbursement, quality assurance, and other purposes. They present three alternatives for dealing with this issue in multiperson therapy, none really satisfactory.

First, professionals can use *DSM-IV* V Codes, which are, by definition, not disorders themselves but may be the focus of treatment. Relational problems specified as V Codes include Relational Problem Related to a Mental Disorder or General Medical Condition, Parent-Child Relational Problem, Partner Relational Problem, Sibling Relational Problem, and Relational Problem Not Otherwise Specified (NOS). Unfortunately, insurers often question the necessity of treating a condition that is not an official mental disorder and generally view such codes as ineligible for reimbursement.

Second, clinicians can assign one family member a *DSM-IV* individual diagnosis of Adjustment Disorder, which is defined as the development of clinically significant emotional or behavioral symptoms in response to an identifiable psychosocial stressor or stressors. When the diagnostic criteria are met, as they frequently are in couple and family therapy, this alternative may be appropriate. However, this strategy requires a psychiatric diagnosis of an individual in the couple or family system, which may misrepresent the nature of the problem and of the therapy. Furthermore, insurers sometimes question the need for treatment of stressful reactions to normal life events.

The third alternative requires providers to assign both a psychiatric diagnosis to an individual and a relational code to describe the family pattern. This approach is acceptable to some insurers and poses no ethical dilemma if the individual diagnosis is accurate. Such an approach may lead to an overemphasis on individual concerns, however, as well as an underemphasis on relational problems. There may also be adverse consequences for the diagnosed individual with respect to employment, future insurance coverage, custody hearings, or other important matters. Given the inadequacy of each of these alternatives, Patterson and Lusterman argue the case for relational assessment, treatment, and reimbursement.

Returning to the Hogan family, how might Dr. Montoya proceed? During Peter's hospitalization, services for his parents can be incorporated into his treatment plan, a strategy that is both clinically and empirically sound. Peter's *DSM-IV* diagnosis is likely to reduce problems with reimbursement. In contrast, following Peter's release, let us assume that his parents continue their participation in the family support group, the multifamily psychoeducational program, and family consultation. From the perspective of diagnosis and reimbursement, the three services have quite different implications.

Because the support group is available without charge from the local NAMI affiliate, questions about diagnosis and reimbursement don't arise. Those questions do arise in connection with family psychoeducation and consultation, both of which are professional services. In the case of psychoeducation, if Peter continues to receive outpatient treatment from the hospital, a strong case can be made for including this family intervention in his treatment plan. Potential benefits for Peter include a reduced risk of relapse and rehospitalization, an outcome that offers financial incentives for his insurer. In contrast, family consultation is typically not reimbursable. Thus, the cost of this service is likely to be shouldered by the Hogans. If they cannot afford consultative services, they may need to forego this intervention unless reduced fees can be negotiated with the provider.

SUGGESTIONS FOR PRACTITIONERS

There are many resources and strategies that can enhance professional practice with families of patients who have serious mental illness. For example, practitioners can:

- attend continuing education programs about serious mental illness and family concerns;
- familiarize themselves with relevant professional publications;
- learn about local services and resources;
- contact their local NAMI affiliate and offer to provide consultation and programs;
- attend state and national NAMI conventions, which offer excellent programs on serious mental illness;
- obtain supervision or consultation from a practitioner who has expertise in the area;
- begin networking with other professionals who share their interests; and
- contact their professional organization to locate relevant programs.

NOTES

WORKING WITH FAMILIES

1. National Advisory Mental Health Council, 1993.
2. Lehman, Steinwachs, and the Co-Investigtors of the PORT Project, 1998.
3. Prevalence data reported in Kessler et al., 1996; Friedman et al., 1996.
4. Experiential quotes not otherwise referenced are based on interviews and surveys published in Marsh, 1992, 1998; Marsh & Dickens, 1997; and Marsh et al., 1996.
5. Dixon, Adams, & Lucksted, 2000; Dixon & Lehman, 1995.
6. Dixon & Lehman, 1995; Falloon et al., 1998.
7. Amenson, 1998b; Torrey, 1995.
8. Marsh, 1992, 1998; Marsh & Johnson, 1997.
9. For discussions of family engagement, see Bernheim & Lehman, 1985; Mueser & Glynn, 1999.
10. For discussions of family assessment, see Bernheim & Lehman, 1985; Mueser & Glynn, 1999.
11. For discussions of the family service plan, see Bernheim, 1994a, 1994b.

PROMOTING RECOVERY AND PREVENTING RELAPSE

1. For a discussion of the vulnerability-stress model, see Mueser & Glynn, 1999.
2. Amenson, 1998a, 1998b, 1998c.
3. Torrey, 1995.
4. Miklowitz & Goldstein, 1997.
5. Falloon et al., 1998.
6. Lefley, 1996.
7. Falloon et al., 1998.
8. For some excellent personal accounts, see Spaniol, Gagne, & Koehler, 1997.
9. Deegan, 1997a, p. 74.
10. Walsh, 1999, p. 58.
11. Gagne, 1999.
12. Wasylenki, 1992.
13. See Harding, Zubin, & Strauss, 1992; Torrey, 1995.
14. Jamison, 1995; Styron, 1990.
15. Walsh, 1999, p. 58.
16. Deegan, 1997b, p. 97.
17. Falloon et al., 1998.

18. For example, see Goodwin & Jamison, 1990; Miklowitz & Goldstein, 1997.
19. Substance Abuse and Mental Health Services Administration, 1994.
20. Kessler et al., 1996.
21. Lehman et al., 1998.
22. Moller & Murphy, 1997.
23. Amenson, 1998a.
24. Falloon et al., 1998.
25. Amenson, 1998a.
26. Amenson, 1998a.
27. Copeland, 1994; Miklowitz & Goldstein, 1997; Moller & Murphy, 1997; Mueser & Glynn, 1999; Weiden, 1997.

THE FAMILY EXPERIENCE OF MENTAL ILLNESS

1. Lefley, 1996.
2. Marsh, 1998.
3. Lefley, 1996.
4. Torrey, 1995.
5. Torrey, 1995.
6. Torrey, 1995.
7. Lefley, 1996.
8. Marsh, 1998.
9. Marsh, 1998.
10. Lehman et al., 1998.
11. Lefley, 1996.
12. Marsh et al., 1996.
13. Figures from U. S. Bureau of the Census, *Statistical Abstract of the U.S.*, 1995.
14. Kazdin, Stolar, & Marciano, 1995.
15. Plummer, 1996.
16. Finley, 1997.
17. Finley, 1997, 2000.
18. Jordan, Lewellen, & Vandiver, 1995.
19. Finley, 1997.
20. Spaniol & Zipple, 1997.
21. Marsh, 1992.
22. For a discussion of phase theories, see Marsh, 1992.
23. Rando, 1984.
24. Marsh & Dickens, 1997.
25. For discussions of family effectiveness, see Figley, 1989; Marsh, 1998.
26. For a discussion of the impact of childhood disability on family functioning, see A. P. Turnbull & H. R. Turnbull, 1990.
27. For a discussion of family appraisal, see Marsh, 1998.
28. Moltz, 1993.
29. Figley, 1989.

DEVELOPING FAMILY-FOCUSED SERVICES

1. Family services have been discussed in more detail in Marsh, 1998.
2. Solomon, 1996.

3. For a comparison of family interventions, see Amenson, 1993; Dixon & Lehman, 1995; Lefley, 1996; Mueser, 1996; Solomon, 1996.
4. Dixon et al., 2000; Dixon & Lehman, 1995.
5. Bernheim, 1994a, 1994b.
6. Amenson, 1998c; Lefley & Wasow,1994; Marsh, 1998; Meisel & Mannion, 1990; Miklowitz & Goldstein, 1997; Mueser & Glynn, 1999; Spaniol et al., 2000.
7. Copeland, 1994; Marsh & Dickens, 1997; Mondimore, 1999; Mueser & Gingerich, 1994; D. F. Papolos & J. Papolos, 1997; Torrey, 1995; Wasow, 1995; Woolis, 1992.
8. Amenson, 1998b, 1998c.
9. Discussed in more detail in Marsh, 1992, 1998.
10. Rolland, 1988, 1994.
11. Rolland, 1988.
12. Reported in Marsh & Dickens, 1997.
13. For discussion of genetic risks, see Gottesman, 1991; Miklowitz & Goldstein, 1997; Torrey, 1995.
14. For example, Radke-Yarrow et al., 1992; Walker & Downey, 1990.
15. Adapted from Marsh, 1998, p. 81.
16. Carter & McGoldrick, 1988.
17. Rolland, 1994.
18. Presented in Marsh, 1998.

FAMILY INTERVENTIONS

1. All of these interventions have been discussed in more detail in Marsh, 1998.
2. Bernheim, 1989; Wynne, McDaniel, & Weber, 1987.
3. Adapted from Marsh, 1998, p. 139.
4. Adapted from Marsh, 1998, pp. 146-148.
5. See Marsh, 1998.
6. Marsh, 1998.
7. Adapted from Marsh, 1998, p. 165.
8. Dixon et al., 2000; Dixon & Lehman, 1995.
9. Mueser & Glynn, 1999.
10. Mueser & Glynn, 1999.
11. Miklowitz & Goldstein, 1997.
12. Marsh & Dickens, 1997.
13. Rodman, 1986, p. 181.

WORKING WITH INDIVIDUAL FAMILY MEMBERS

1. Professional practice with parents, spouses, siblings, and offspring has been discussed in more detail in Marsh, 1998.
2. Lefley, 1996.
3. For a discussion of the impact of a child's disability on marital relations, see Featherstone, 1980.
4. Taylor et al., 2000.
5. Judge, 1994; Mannion, 1996; The Well Spouse Foundation in San Diego estimates that 7 to 9 million spouses are living with partners who have serious mental illness (cited in Wasow, 1995).

6. Experiential quotes from spouses largely taken from their suggestions for the chapter on spouses in Marsh, 1998.
7. Marsh, 1998; Wasow, 1995.
8. See Judge, 1994; Mannion, 1996; Wasow, 1995.
9. Mannion, 1998.
10. Bayes, 1997.
11. Gallo, 1988.
12. For a discussion of these issues in connection with sibling disability, see Powell & Gallagher, 1993.
13. Poznanski, 1972.
14. Goode, 1989, p. 63.
15. Weisburd, 1992, p. 13.
16. Kelley, 1992, p. 28.
17. Anthony, 1975; Guttman, 1989.
18. Oakes, 1996, pp. 42-43.
19. Anthony & Cohler, 1987.
20. Mannion, 1996, 1998.
21. Mannion & Meisel, 1993.
22. Rice, 1994.
23. Mannion, in Marsh, 1998.
24. See model programs in Marsh, 1998.
25. Kinsella, 1996, p. 58.
26. Wasow, 1995.
27. Wasow, 1995, p. 16.
28. Marsh & Dickens, 1997.

COPING WITH CHALLENGES

1. Discussed in more detail in Marsh, 1998.
2. Mondimore, 1999; Mueser & Gingerich, 1994; Torrey, 1995.
3. Regier et al., 1990.
4. Bernheim & Lehman, 1985.
5. Woolis, 1992.
6. McDaniel, Hepworth, & Doherty, 1993; quote from p. 62.
7. Bernheim & Lehman, 1985, p. 175.
8. Bernheim & Lehman, 1985, p. 187.

PROFESSIONAL ISSUES

1. Hansen & Goldberg, 1999.
2. American Psychological Association, 1992.
3. Marsh & Magee, 1997.
4. See Hansen & Goldberg, 1999.
5. See Marsh, 1998.
6. See Marsh, 1998; Zipple et al., 1997.
7. Kaslow, 1993.
8. American Psychiatric Association, 1994.
9. Kaslow, 1996.
10. Patterson & Lusterman, 1996.

REFERENCES

Amenson, C. S. (1993). *Education, Consultation and Treatment of Families With a Mentally Ill Member: A Guide for Effective Professional Intervention.* Pasadena, CA: Pacific Clinics Institute.

Amenson, C. S. (1998a). *Family Skills in Relapse Prevention.* Pasadena, CA: Pacific Clinics Institute.

Amenson, C. S. (1998b). *Schizophrenia: A Family Education Curriculum.* Pasadena, CA: Pacific Clinics Institute.

Amenson, C. S. (1998c). *Schizophrenia: Family Education Methods.* Pasadena, CA: Pacific Clinics Institute.

American Psychiatric Association. (1994). *Diagnostic and Statistical Manual of Mental Disorders* (4th ed.). Washington, DC: Author.

American Psychological Association. (1992). Ethical principles of psychologists and code of conduct. *American Psychologist, 47,* 1597-1611.

Anthony, E. J. (1975). The influence of a manic-depressive environment on the developing child. In E. J. Anthony & T. Benedek (Eds.), *Depression and Human Existence* (pp. 279-315). Boston: Little, Brown.

Anthony, E. J., & Cohler, B. J. (Eds.). (1987). *The Invulnerable Child.* New York: Guilford.

Bayes, K. A. (1997, July). *Meeting the Needs of Spouses.* Paper presented at the annual meeting of NAMI, Albuquerque, NM.

Bernheim, K. F. (1989). Psychologists and families of the severely mentally ill: The role of family consultation. *American Psychologist, 44,* 561-564.

Bernheim, K. F. (1994a). Determining and implementing the family service plan. In H. Lefley & M. Wasow (Eds.), *Helping Families Cope With Mental Illness* (pp. 147-160). Newark, NJ: Harwood Academic.

Bernheim, K. F. (1994b). Skills and strategies for working with families. In D. T. Marsh (Ed.), *New Directions in the Psychological Treatment of Serious Mental Illness* (pp. 186-198). Westport, CT: Praeger.

Bernheim, K. F., & Lehman, A. F. (1985). *Working With Families of the Mentally Ill.* New York: Norton.

Carter, B., & McGoldrick, M. (Eds.). (1988). *The Changing Family Life Cycle* (2nd ed.). New York: Gardner.

Copeland, M. E. (1994). *Living Without Depression and Manic Depression: A Workbook for Maintaining Mood Stability.* Oakland CA: New Harbinger.

Deegan, P. E. (1997a). Recovery as a journey of the heart. In L. Spaniol, C. Gagne, & M. Koehler (Eds.), *Psychological and Social Aspects of Psychiatric Disability* (pp. 74-83). Boston: Boston University Center for Psychiatric Rehabilitation.

Deegan, P. E. (1997b). Recovery: The lived experience of rehabilitation. In L. Spaniol, C. Gagne, & M. Koehler (Eds.), *Psychological and Social Aspects of Psychiatric Disability* (pp. 92-98). Boston: Boston University Center for Psychiatric Rehabilitation.

Dixon, L. B., Adams, C., & Lucksted, A. (2000). Update on family psychoeducation for schizophrenia. *Schizophrenia Bulletin, 26,* 5-20.

Dixon, L. B., & Lehman A. F. (1995). Family interventions for schizophrenia. *Schizophrenia Bulletin, 21,* 631-643.

Falloon, I. R. H., Roncone, R., Malm, U., & Coverdale, J. H. (1998). Effective and efficient treatment strategies to enhance recovery from schizophrenia: How much longer will people have to wait before we provide them? *Psychiatric Rehabilitation Skills, 2,* 107-127.

Featherstone, H. (1980). *A Difference in the Family: Living With a Disabled Child.* New York: Penguin.

Figley, C. R. (1989). *Helping Traumatized Families.* San Francisco: Jossey-Bass.

Finley, L. Y. (1997). The multiple effects of culture and ethnicity on psychiatric disability. In L. Spaniol, C. Gagne, & M. Koehler (Eds.),

Psychological and Social Aspects of Psychiatric Disability (pp. 497-510). Boston: Boston University Center for Psychiatric Rehabilitation.

Finley, L. Y. (2000). The cultural context: Families coping with psychiatric disability. In L. Spaniol, A. M. Zipple, D. T. Marsh, & L. Y. Finley (Eds.), *The Role of the Family in Psychiatric Rehabilitation: A Workbook* (pp. 159-186). Boston: Boston University Center for Psychiatric Rehabilitation.

Friedman, R. M., Katz-Leavy, J. W., Manderscheid, R. W., & Sondheimer, D. L. (1996). Prevalence of serious emotional disturbance in children and adolescents. In R. W. Manderscheid & M. A. Sonnenschein (Eds.), *Mental Health, United States, 1996* (pp. 71-89) (DHHS Publication No. SMA 96-3098). Washington, DC: U.S. Government Printing Office.

Gagne, C. (1999, August). *Recovery from Mental Illness: Results from the Recovery Research Project.* Paper presented at the annual meeting of the American Psychological Association, Boston, MA.

Gallo, A. M. (1988). The special sibling relationship in chronic illness and disability: Parental communication with well siblings. *Holistic Nursing Practice, 2,* 28-37.

Goode, E. E. (1989, April 24). When mental illness hits home. *U.S. News & World Report,* pp. 55-57, 60, 62-65.

Goodwin, F. K., & Jamison, K. R. (1990). *Manic Depressive Illness.* New York: Oxford University Press.

Gottesman, I. I. (1991). *Schizophrenia Genesis: The Origins of Madness.* New York: Freeman.

Guttman, H. A. (1989). Children in families with emotionally disturbed parents. In L. Combrinck-Graham (Ed.), *Children in Family Contexts: Perspectives on Treatment* (pp. 252-276). New York: Guilford.

Hansen, N. D., & Goldberg, S. G. (1999). Navigating the nuances: A matrix of considerations for ethical-legal dilemmas. *Professional Psychology: Research and Practice, 30,* 495-503.

Harding, C. M., Zubin, J., & Strauss, J. S. (1992). Chronicity in schizophrenia: Revisited. *British Journal of Psychiatry, 161,* 27-37.

Jamison, K. R. (1995). *An Unquiet Mind: A Memoir of Moods and Madness.* New York: Knopf.

Jordan, C., Lewellen, A., & Vandiver, V. (1995). Psychoeducation for minority families: A social work perspective. *International Journal of Mental Health, 23,* 27-43.

Judge, K. (1994). Serving children, siblings, and spouses: Understanding the needs of other family members. In H. P. Lefley & M. Wasow (Eds.), *Helping Families Cope With Mental Illness* (pp. 161-194). Newark, NJ: Harwood Academic.

Kaslow, F. W. (1993). Relational diagnosis: Past, present and future. *American Journal of Family Therapy, 21,* 195-204.

Kaslow, F. W. (Ed.). (1996). *Handbook of Relational Diagnosis and Dysfunctional Family Patterns.* New York: Wiley.

Kazdin, A. E., Stolar, M. J., & Marciano, P. L. (1995). Risk factors for dropping out of treatment among white and black families. *Journal of Family Psychology, 9,* 402-417.

Kelley, W. (1992). Unmet needs. *The JOURNAL of the California Alliance for the Mentally Ill, 3*(1), 28.

Kessler, R. C., Berglund, P. A., Zhao, S., Leaf, P. J., Kouzis, A. C., Bruce, M. L., Friedman, R. M., Grosser, R. C., Kennedy, C., Narrow, W. E., Kuehnel, T. G., Laska, E. M., Manderscheid, R. W., Rosenheck, R. A., Santoni, T. W., & Schneier, M. (1996). The 12-month prevalence and correlates of serious mental illness (SMI). In R. W. Manderscheid & M. A. Sonnenschein (Eds.), *Mental Health, United States, 1996* (pp. 59-70) (DHHS Publication No. SMA 96-3098). Washington, DC: U.S. Government Printing Office.

Kinsella, K. (1996). Helping children cope. *The JOURNAL of the California Alliance for the Mentally Ill, 7*(3), 58-59.

Lefley, H. P. (1996). *Family Caregiving in Mental Illness* (Family Caregiver Applications Series, Vol. 7). Thousand Oaks, CA: Sage.

Lefley, H. P., & Wasow, M. (Eds.). (1994). *Helping Families Cope With Mental Illness.* Newark, NJ: Harwood Academic.

Lehman, A. F., Steinwachs, D. M., & the Co-Investigators of the PORT Project. (1998). At issue: Translating research into practice: The Schizophrenia Patient Outcomes Research Team (PORT) treatment recommendations. *Schizophrenia Bulletin, 24,* 1-10.

Mannion, E. (1996). Resilience and burden in spouses of people with mental illness. *Psychiatric Rehabilitation Journal, 20*(2), 13-23.

Mannion, E. (1998). The ultimate acrobats. *The JOURNAL of the California Alliance for the Mentally Ill. 9*(2), 72-76.

Mannion, E., & Meisel, M. (1993). *Teaching Manual for Spouse Coping Skills Workshops.* Philadelphia, PA: Training and Educational Center (TEC) Network, c/o Mental Health Association of Southeastern Pennsylvania.

Marsh, D. T. (1992). *Families and Mental Illness: New Directions in Professional Practice.* New York: Praeger.

Marsh, D. T. (1998). *Serious Mental Illness and the Family: The Practitioner's Guide.* New York: Wiley.

Marsh, D. T., & Dickens, R. M. (1997). *Troubled Journey: Coming to Terms With the Mental Illness of a Sibling or Parent.* New York: Tarcher/Putnam.

Marsh, D. T., & Johnson, D. L. (1997). The family experience of mental illness: Implications for intervention. *Professional Psychology: Research and Practice, 28,* 229-237.

Marsh, D. T., Lefley, H. P., Evans-Rhodes, D., Ansell, V. I., Doerzbacher, B. M., LaBarbera, L., & Paluzzi, J. E. (1996). The family experience of mental illness: Evidence for resilience. *Psychiatric Rehabilitation Journal, 20*(2), 3-12.

Marsh, D. T., & Magee, R. D. (Eds.). (1997). *Ethical and Legal Issues in Professional Practice With Families.* New York: Wiley.

McDaniel, S. H., Hepworth, J., & Doherty, W. J. (1993, January/February). A new prescription for family health care. *Family Networker, 17*(2), 18-29, 62-63.

Meisel, M., & Mannion, E. (1990). *Teaching Manual for Coping Skills Workshops* (rev. ed.). Philadelphia, PA: Training and Educational Center (TEC) Network, c/o Mental Health Association of Southeastern Pennsylvania.

Miklowitz, D. J., & Goldstein, M. J. (1997). *Bipolar Disorder: A Family-Focused Treatment Approach.* New York: Guilford.

Moller, M. D., & Murphy, M. F. (1997). The Three R's Rehabilitation Program: A prevention approach for the management of relapse symptoms associated with psychiatric diagnoses. *Psychiatric Rehabilitation Journal, 20*(3), 42-48.

Moltz, D. A. (1993). Bipolar disorder and the family: An integrative model. *Family Process, 32,* 409-423.

Mondimore, F. M. (1999). *Bipolar Disorder: A Guide for Patients and Families.* Baltimore: Johns Hopkins.

Mueser, K. T. (1996). Helping families manage severe mental illness. *Psychiatric Rehabilitation Skills, 1*(2), 21-42.

Mueser, K. T., & Gingerich, S. (1994). *Coping With Schizophrenia: A Guide for Families.* Oakland, CA: New Harbinger.

Mueser, K. T., & Glynn, S. M. (1999). *Behavioral Family Therapy for Psychiatric Disorders* (2nd ed.). Oakland, CA: New Harbinger.

National Advisory Mental Health Council. (1993). Health care reform for Americans with severe mental illnesses. *American Journal of Psychiatry, 150,* 1447-1465.

Oakes, B. (1996). The static bond: A daughter's experience with her mother's mental illness. *The JOURNAL of the California Alliance for the Mentally Ill, 7*(3), 42-43.

Papolos, D. F., & Papolos, J. (1997). *Overcoming Depression* (3rd ed.). New York: HarperCollins.

Patterson, T. E., & Lusterman, D-D. (1996). The relational reimbursement dilemma. In F. W. Kaslow (Ed.), *Handbook of Relational Diagnosis and Dysfunctional Family Patterns* (pp. 46-58). New York: Wiley.

Plummer, D. L. (1996). Developing culturally responsive psychosocial rehabilitative programs for African Americans. *Psychiatric Rehabilitation Journal, 19*(4), 37-43.

Powell, T. H., & Gallagher, P. (1993). *Brothers & Sisters: A Special Part of Exceptional Families* (2nd ed.). Baltimore: Paul H. Brookes.

Poznanski, E. O. (1972). The "replacement child": A saga of unresolved parental grief. *Journal of Pediatrics, 81,* 1190-1193.

Radke-Yarrow, M., Nottelmann, E., Martinez, P., Fox, M. B., & Belmont, B. (1992). Young children of affectively ill parents: A longitudinal study of psychosocial development. *Journal of the American Academy of Child & Adolescent Psychiatry, 31,* 68-77.

Rando, T. A. (1984). *Grief, Dying, and Death: Clinical Interventions for Caregivers.* Champaign, IL: Research Press.

Regier, D. A., Farmer, M. E., Rae, D. S., Locke, B. Z., Keith, S. J., Judd, L. L., & Goodwin, F. K. (1990). Comorbidity of mental disorders with alcohol and other drug abuse: Results from the Epidemiologic Catchment Area (ECA) Study. *Journal of the American Medical Association, 264,* 2511-2518.

Rice, J. (1994, September). *New Roles for Psychiatrists With Members of Patients' Families: Parents, Spouses, and Siblings.* Paper presented at the Psychiatry Grand Round of Jefferson Medical College Department of Psychiatry, Philadelphia, PA.

Rodman, F. R. (1986). *Keeping Hope Alive: On Becoming a Psychotherapist.* New York: Harper & Row.

Rolland, J. S. (1988). Chronic illness and the family life cycle. In B. Carter & M. McGoldrick (Eds.), *The Changing Family Life Cycle* (2nd ed., pp. 433-456). New York: Gardner.

Rolland, J. S. (1994). *Families, Illness, and Disability: An Integrative Treatment Model.* New York: Basic Books.

Solomon, P. (1996). Moving from psychoeducation to family education for families of adults with serious mental illness. *Psychiatric Services, 47,* 1364-1370.

Spaniol, L., Gagne, C., & Koehler, M. (Eds.). (1997). *Psychological and Social Aspects of Psychiatric Disability.* Boston: Boston University Center for Psychiatric Rehabilitation.

Spaniol, L., & Zipple, A. M. (1997). The family recovery process. In L. Spaniol, C. Gagne, & M. Koehler (Eds.), *Psychological and Social Aspects of Psychiatric Disability* (pp. 281-284). Boston: Boston University Center for Psychiatric Rehabilitation.

Spaniol, L., Zipple, A. M., Marsh, D. T., & Finley, L. Y. (Eds.). (2000). *The Role of the Family in Psychiatric Rehabilitation: A Workbook.* Boston: Boston University Center for Psychiatric Rehabilitation.

Styron, W. (1990). *Darkness Visible: A Memoir of Madness.* New York: Random House.

Substance Abuse and Mental Health Services Administration. (1994). *Cost of Addictive and Mental Disorders and Effectiveness of Treatment* (DHHS Publication No. SMA 2095-94). Washington, DC: U.S. Government Printing Office.

Taylor, S. E., Klein, L. C., Lewis, B. P., Gruenewald, T. L., Gurung, R. A. R., & Updegraff, J. A. (2000). Biobehavioral responses to stress in females: Tend-and-befriend, not fight-or-flight. *Psychological Review, 107,* 411-429.

Torrey, E. F. (1995). *Surviving Schizophrenia: A Manual for Families, Consumers and Providers* (3rd ed.). New York: HarperCollins.

Turnbull, A. P., & Turnbull, H. R. (1990). *Families, Professionals, and Exceptionality: A Special Partnership* (2nd ed.). Columbus, OH: Merrill.

U.S. Bureau of the Census. (1995). *Statistical Abstract of the U.S.* Washington, DC: U.S. Government Printing Office.

Walker, E. F., & Downey, G. (1990). The effects of familial risk factors on social-cognitive abilities in children. *Child Psychiatry and Human Development, 20,* 253-267.

Walsh, D. (1999). Coping with a journey toward recovery: From the inside out. In R. P. Marinelli & A. E. Dell Orto (Eds.), *The Psychological and Social Impact of Disability* (4th ed., pp. 55-61). New York: Springer.

Wasow, M. (1995). *The Skipping Stone: Ripple Effects of Mental Illness on the Family.* Palo Alto, CA: Science & Behavior Books.

Wasylenki, D. A. (1992). Psychotherapy of schizophrenia revisited. *Hospital and Community Psychiatry, 43,* 123-127.

Weiden, P. J. (Ed.). (1997). *Team Care Solutions.* Indianapolis, IN: Eli Lilly & Co.

Weisburd, S. B. (1992). Adapting to the changed relationship: One sibling's perspective. *The JOURNAL of the California Alliance for the Mentally Ill, 3*(1), 13-15.

Woolis, R. (1992). *When Someone You Love Has a Mental Illness.* New York: Tarcher/Perigee.

Wynne, L. C., McDaniel, S. H., & Weber, T. T. (1987). Professional politics and the concepts of family therapy, family consultation, and systems consultation. *Family Process, 26,* 153-166.

Zipple, A. M., Langle, S., Tyrell, W., Spaniol, L., & Fisher, H. (1997). Client confidentiality and the family's need to know: Strategies for resolving the conflict. In D. T. Marsh & R. D. Magee (Eds.), *Ethical and Legal Issues in Professional Practice With Families* (pp. 238-253). New York: Wiley.

EARN 3 HOME STUDY CONTINUING EDUCATION CREDITS*

Professional Resource Exchange, Inc. offers a 3-credit home study continuing education program as a supplement to this book. For information, please return this form, call 1-800-443-3364, fax to 941-343-9201, write to the address below, or visit our website: http://www.prpress.com

*The Professional Resource Exchange, Inc., is approved by the American Psychological Association to offer Continuing Education for psychologists. The Professional Resource Exchange maintains responsibility for the program. We are also recognized by the National Board for Certified Counselors to offer continuing education for National Certified Counselors. We adhere to NBCC Continuing Education Guidelines (Provider #5474). Home study CE programs are accepted by most state licensing boards. Please consult your board, however, if you have questions regarding that body's acceptance of structured home study programs offered by APA-approved sponsors. Our programs have also been specifically approved for MFCCs and LCSWs in California and MFTs, LCSWs, and MHCs in Florida.

Name: _____
(Please Print)

Address: _____

Address: _____

City/State/Zip: _____
This is ☐ home ☐ office

Telephone: (_____)_____

I am a:

☐ Psychologist   ☐ Mental Health Counselor
☐ Psychiatrist   ☐ Marriage and Family Therapist
☐ School Psychologist   ☐ Not in Mental Health Field
☐ Clinical Social Worker   ☐ Other: _____

Professional Resource Press
P.O. Box 15560
Sarasota, FL 34277-1560

Telephone: 800-443-3364
FAX: 941-343-9201
E-mail: mail@prpress.com
Website: http://www.prpress.com

Add A Colleague To Our Mailing List . . .

If you would like us to send our latest catalog to one of your colleagues, please return this form:

Name: _____
(Please Print)

Address: _____

Address: _____

City/State/Zip: _____
This is ☐ home ☐ office

Telephone: (_____) _____

This person is a:

☐ Psychologist   ☐ Mental Health Counselor
☐ Psychiatrist   ☐ Marriage and Family Therapist
☐ School Psychologist   ☐ Not in Mental Health Field
☐ Clinical Social Worker   ☐ Other: _____

Name of person completing this form: _____

◆   ◆   ◆

Professional Resource Press
P.O. Box 15560
Sarasota, FL 34277-1560

Telephone: 800-443-3364
FAX: 941-343-9201
E-mail: mail@prpress.com
Website: http://www.prpress.com

FFA/12/00(SMI)